Study Skills 1

STUDY SKILLS

SADDLEBACK
EDUCATIONAL PUBLISHING

STUDY SKILLS

Study Skills 1

Study Skills 2

SADDLEBACK
EDUCATIONAL PUBLISHING
www.sdlback.com

ISBN-13: 978-1-62250-022-2
ISBN-10: 1-62250-022-9
eBook: 978-1-61247-665-0

Printed in the United States of America

17 16 15 14 13   1 2 3 4 5

CONTENTS

A LEARNING SKILLS INVENTORY

You probably have some good study skills already. Are you aware of which skills need improvement?

A. Think about your current skill levels. Check one box after each skill area. Be honest! Identifying your strengths and

weaknesses is the first step toward becoming a better student.

	EXCELLENT	GOOD	FAIR	POOR
1. Reading speed				
2. Reading comprehension				
3. Listening				
4. Memory				
5. Following directions				
6. Time management				
7. Textbook note-taking				
8. Classroom note-taking				
9. Class discussion participation				
10. Relations with instructors				
11. Basic library skills				
12. Writing papers				
13. Test preparation				
14. Test taking				

B. Use information from your checklist to answer each question.

1. Name the study skills area that you now feel most confident about.

   _____

2. Name the study skills area in which you most need improvement.

   _____

C. On the back of this sheet, list your classes. Write the instructor's name after each class. How hard do you find each class? Rate the levels of difficulty from 1 (least difficult) to 5 (most difficult).

STUDY SKILLS VOCABULARY

Certain ways of doing things make learning easier. These ways are called *learning methods* or *study skills.* Strong study skills can be a big help at school. In fact, they can make you a better learner at any time or place in your life.

A. The 10 words below are important to learn. Write a letter to match each word on the left with its definition on the right.

1. ____ directions

2. ____ notes

3. ____ organize

4. ____ preview

5. ____ review

6. ____ memorize

7. ____ practice

8. ____ comprehend

9. ____ textbook

10. ____ cram

a. to go back and look over material *after* an earlier reading

b. to look over information *before* a more careful reading

c. to study only the night before a test or at the last minute

d. to fix in your mind or learn by heart

e. a book used to teach a school subject

f. to do something over and over again

g. to fully understand something

h. instructions on how to do something

i. to put things in order, according to a system

j. something you write to help you remember or keep track

B. Circle ten hidden words in the puzzle. They may go up, down, across, backward, or diagonally. Check off each word as you find it in the puzzle.

____ DIRECTIONS   ____ ORGANIZE

____ PREVIEW   ____ REVIEW

____ MEMORIZE   ____ PRACTICE

____ COMPREHEND   ____ CRAM

____ NOTES   ____ TEXTBOOK

```
P C O M P R E H E N D X N
G R T B O R G A N I Z E O
L A E R T U A P E R W R T
T M K V A G O C O R I A E
W N A D I R E C T I O N S
O R E V I E W O G I A W Y
M T R M B C W F L A C M C
Q Y H N M E M O R I Z E S
K O O B T X E T Y A L Z B
```

    Study Skills 1 • © Saddleback Educational Publishing • www.sdlback.com

A GOOD STUDY ENVIRONMENT

Do you have a good place to study? The things that surround you when you learn make up your *study environment.* Where and how you set up a place to study can affect the quality of your learning.

A. Circle a letter to identify the best learning environment. Then list some features of the better environment that would aid learning.

    a. Jason is ready to study. He sits in a soft chair in the living room. The glow of the TV lights his history book. His sister is watching a science fiction movie. Jason puts on stereo headphones to block the TV noise. When it's time to answer questions, Jason looks around for a pen and paper.

    b. Lynn is ready to study. She carries a glass of water to her room. She closes her door and turns on the light over the table. She takes a dictionary, a pen, and some paper from a shelf. Today, Lynn will read a history chapter and answer questions. She checks her watch. It is 4:30 P.M., an hour before dinner.

    FEATURES OF THE BETTER ENVIRONMENT: _____

_____

_____

B. Evaluate your usual study area. Write **yes** or **no** for each question.

    1. ____ Do you have one or two places reserved just for studying?

    2. ____ Is your study area where others will not pass through?

    3. ____ Is your whole desk or table well lit?

    4. ____ Can you avoid outside noise by closing the door?

    5. ____ Do you usually study before you are tired?

    6. ____ Are your study materials near the work area?

    7. ____ Is your work area cool (but not cold)—between 65° and 70°?

    8. ____ Do you sit upright when you study?

C. Review your answers to the questions in *Part B.* On the back of this sheet, list ways you could improve your own study environment.

TIME MANAGEMENT: TRACKING YOUR TIME

Are you a good time manager? Or do you scramble to
get schoolwork done at the last minute? You may need
to take better control of your time!

A. Look at the time log below. List the activities you
usually perform during a school day. Write down the
approximate time of day you perform each activity
and guess how long you spend on each one. Make
sure your log shows a 24-hour period. Include hours
spent dressing, eating, getting to and from school,
watching TV, talking on the phone, and sleeping.
If you need more space, use the back of this sheet.

ACTIVITY	TIME OF DAY	TIME SPENT	ACTIVITY	TIME OF DAY	TIME SPENT

B. Study the information in your log. Write the amount of time spent
on each of the following activities.

1. personal grooming _____

2. meals _____

3. attending school _____

4. jobs _____

5. TV _____

6. studying _____

7. recreation with friends _____

8. relaxing alone _____

9. sports _____

10. talking on the phone _____

11. other activities _____

12. sleeping _____

C. Answer these questions on the back of this sheet: (1) Do you see any
use of time that surprises you? If so, explain. (2) What is one change
in your schedule that might help you use your time more wisely?

Study Skills 1 • © Saddleback Educational Publishing • www.sdlback.com

TIME MANAGEMENT: PLANNING YOUR TIME

Planning a daily schedule will help you manage time better. How? By making clear what you *must* do so you will have time for things you *want* to do. A schedule is a tool meant to help, not control, you. You can always adjust your schedule if you need to.

A. Circle a letter to show which words best complete each sentence.

1. I consider my *prime time* (when I'm most awake and alert) to be

   a. morning.   c. evening.

   b. afternoon.   d. late night.

2. I learn better by studying for

   a. a few long periods with short breaks.

   b. many short periods with long breaks.

3. I believe I need to set aside study time

   a. every day.   b. most days.   c. only a few days a week.

4. On a day when I have no regular homework, I usually

   a. skip studying.   b. work on long-term assignments.   c. read.

B. On the back of this sheet, list your *obligations*—things you must do—for your next school day. Include classes, job, sports practice, club meetings, etc.

C. Plan your next school day on the daily schedule below. See the list from *Part B* for things you **must** do. Then think about things you **want** to do. Consider your prime time for study. Schedule free time to relax.

Date: _____
(Write the date of the next school day here.)

6:00 A.M.	3:00
7:00	4:00
8:00	5:00
9:00	6:00
10:00	7:00
11:00	8:00
12:00	9:00
1:00 P.M.	10:00
2:00	11:00

THINKING ABOUT LEARNING STYLE

People learn in many different ways. Some people like to read about something before they try it. Others learn best by jumping right in and actually doing the thing. Some people like to be told about a new thing or watch others do it first. Think about your own favorite way to learn. The way you learn best is called your *learning style.*

A. On the line below, write an activity you learned to do or a topic you learned about within this past year. (Examples of activities: playing an instrument, snowboarding. Examples of topics: the Grand Canyon, the U.S. Constitution.)

_____

B. What methods did you use to learn the topic or activity that you named in *Part A*? Check all the words or phrases that describe your methods.

____ reading   ____ watching others

____ memorizing   ____ learning in a class

____ listening to an instructor   ____ learning with a group of friends

____ practicing on my own   ____ writing or taking notes

____ watching movies or videos   ____ drawing pictures and diagrams

____ listening to tapes   ____ looking at charts and graphs

____ following written directions   ____ following spoken instructions

C. Name an activity or subject you would like to learn in this next year. Write it on the line.

_____

D. How will you go about learning your new activity or subject? Write a plan for learning on the back of this sheet. List some of the learning methods from *Part B* as well as any other methods that would work best for *you.*

IDENTIFYING YOUR LEARNING STYLE

If you are an *auditory* learner, you learn best and remember information longer if you hear it. If you are a *visual* learner, you learn best if you see the information or picture it in your head. If you are a *kinesthetic* learner, you learn best by handling materials and *doing* something.

A. Which type of learner would probably prefer each learning method? Write **A** for **auditory**, **V** for **visual**, or **K** for **kinesthetic**.

1. _____ looking at chalkboard diagrams
2. _____ putting on a demonstration
3. _____ studying a map
4. _____ building a model
5. _____ doing an experiment
6. _____ imagining a story character
7. _____ recording information and listening to it
8. _____ going to a lecture
9. _____ repeating information aloud
10. _____ reviewing written notes

B. Most people use more than just one learning style. However, one style is usually stronger than the others. Read the following description. Decide if the student, Carla, is mainly an *auditory, visual,* or *kinesthetic* learner. Write your answer on the line after the paragraph.

> Carla had a hard time in some of her classes. She had trouble finishing the books assigned in English class. She could not concentrate on her history teacher's lectures. But Carla did well at drama and industrial arts. And she liked doing science experiments. One day, the English teacher had students act out scenes from a novel. The story came alive for Carla! Acting out the scenes made the story much more interesting and helped Carla remember details.

Carla's strongest learning style is _____

C. Are you an auditory, visual, or kinesthetic learner? On the back of this sheet, write a paragraph describing your own learning style. Use Carla's story as a model.

KNOW YOUR INSTRUCTOR

Like all people, instructors are different from one another. They have their own teaching styles just as students have their own learning styles. If you "study your teachers," you can meet their expectations more easily and use your study time more wisely.

A. Name the instructor whose class you find most difficult.

INSTRUCTOR: _____   CLASS: _____

Write **T** or **F** to show whether each statement is, in your opinion, a **true** or **false** description of your teacher's expectations.

This teacher:

1. _____ accepts late homework without penalty.

2. _____ instructs mostly with lectures.

3. _____ expects students to participate in discussion.

4. _____ encourages questions.

5. _____ has penalties for tardiness.

6. _____ expects quiet and orderly conduct.

7. _____ puts up with some disorder and disruption.

8. _____ expects students to memorize exact information.

9. _____ accepts and encourages student opinion.

10. _____ expects students to take notes.

11. _____ bases grades mainly on test scores.

12. _____ considers student effort when giving grades.

13. _____ usually spots unprepared students.

14. _____ often gives surprise quizzes.

15. _____ often assigns long-term projects or papers.

16. _____ assigns homework nearly every night.

17. _____ is willing to help outside of class time.

B. On the back of this sheet, write two statements that further describe this person's teaching style. What are his or her expectations for attendance, behavior, homework, and participation? What are his or her methods of grading and testing?

SETTING GOALS

Your goals are aims you hope to achieve.

- *Long-range goals* are aims for the future.
- *Mid-range goals* are aims that will lead to the target—the long-range goal.
- *Short-range goals* are small steps that you can complete in a fairly short period of time.

A *Goal Pyramid* can help you picture these goals.

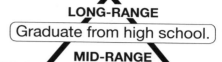

LONG-RANGE
Graduate from high school.

MID-RANGE
Pass U.S. history, world history, and American government.

SHORT-RANGE
Complete U.S. history project, study for final test, sign up for next term's American government class.

A. Make your own goal pyramid. Write the answer to each question on the line that matches the number.

1. What is one thing you would like to accomplish in the next 10 years? *(long-range)*

2. What are some things you must accomplish in the next 2 years to reach your 10-year goal? *(mid-range)*

3. What are some things you must accomplish in the next six months to reach your 2-year goal? *(short-range)*

1. _____
_____

2. _____
_____

3. _____
_____

B. Think of a goal you would like to reach in one month. On the back of this sheet, make a pyramid. Show the long-range goal (one month) plus mid-range (two week) and short-range (daily) steps toward the goal. For example, your pyramid might list steps that would lead to passing a big math text, improving physical fitness, or writing your own blog.

IMPROVING MEMORY

Like any skill, the ability to remember improves with practice. Test your memory skills with this game.

A. Read the list of items in the box. Then cover the list with your hand or a piece of paper. Write all the items you can remember on the lines.

LIST A

window	toothbrush
blanket	crow
nail	radio
laptop	calendar
cheese	train

_____ _____

_____ _____

_____ _____

_____ _____

_____ _____

B. Now read this second list of items. Again, cover the list and write the items you remember on the lines.

LIST B

coat	umbrella
hat	ear muffs
boots	sweater
scarf	hood
gloves	mittens

_____ _____

_____ _____

_____ _____

_____ _____

_____ _____

C. 1. How many items did you correctly recall from *List A*? _____

2. How many items did you correctly recall from *List B*? _____

3. Which list could you most accurately remember? _____

4. Most people will recall more items from *List B*. Why do you think this is? Circle a letter to show the reason.

   a. Items in *List B* are more interesting.

   b. Words in *List B* are shorter.

   c. Items in *List B* all belong to a group or category.

  Study Skills 1 • © Saddleback Educational Publishing • www.sdlback.com

TWO WAYS TO IMPROVE MEMORY

GROUPING

You have learned that it is often easier to remember separate items of information when they are organized into groups or categories.

A. Organize the items below into three groups. Write a title for the category at the top of each list.

sink	bus	banana	bathtub	airplane
orange	peach	mirror	shower	apple
subway	steamship	toilet	grapefruit	truck

GROUP NAME 1:	GROUP NAME 2:	GROUP NAME 3:
_____	_____	_____
ITEMS:	ITEMS:	ITEMS:
_____	_____	_____
_____	_____	_____
_____	_____	_____
_____	_____	_____
_____	_____	_____

VISUALIZING

Mental images also can help you remember data. This means that you translate words and ideas into pictures in your mind.

B. Look around at the room you're in now. Pay attention to details. Then close your eyes and picture the room in your mind. Open your eyes again. How clear was your mental picture? Notice specific items. Then turn over this sheet. Without looking up, list all the details of the room that you can remember. Compare your list with a classmate's to see who recalled the most details.

C. Now combine grouping and visualizing. On the back of this sheet, group details of the room into three main categories.

MNEMONICS: MEMORY BOOSTERS

Have you heard of special memory aids called *mnemonic* **(nee-mon´-ik)** *devices?* These methods can help you recall information more easily.

A mnemonic device known as an *acrostic* can help you remember lists. To create an acrostic, take the first letter from each word that you want to remember. Then create a sentence or phrase in which each word begins with the same letter as the words you want to recall. For example, you might need to memorize the names of the Great Lakes. This acrostic could help you: *Some hungry men eat oatmeal.*

SUPERIOR HURON MICHIGAN ERIE ONTARIO

SOME HUNGRY MEN EAT OATMEAL.

A. Now create an acrostic of your own. Think of a sentence that would help you remember the names of the four largest oceans in the world:

PACIFIC   ATLANTIC   INDIAN   ARCTIC

(Hint: You can put the names of the oceans in any order.)

EXAMPLE: *Pick apples in April.*

Write your acrostic on the line.

PICK BY
APRIL 30!

Here's another mnemonic device that works well and is fun to do. This one involves making up a catchy sentence, phrase, or rhyme containing the information you want to remember. For example, this handy rhyme helps people remember whether the spelling of a word is *i* before *e* or *e* before *i:*

I before *e* except after *c,*
or when sounded like *a* as in *neighbor* or *weigh*.

B. On the back of this sheet, write a rhyme, sentence, or phrase to help you remember the six bands of color in a rainbow (red, orange, yellow, green, blue, and violet).

TEXTBOOKS: Special Features

A textbook has special features to help you learn. Knowing how to find and use all the parts of a textbook can make studying easier.

A. Read the list of textbook parts on the left. Write a letter to match each part with its description on the right.

1. ____ **title page**

2. ____ **copyright page**

3. ____ **table of contents**

4. ____ **glossary**

5. ____ **index**

6. ____ **bibliography**

7. ____ **appendix**

a. chapter-by-chapter list of the book's contents; appears at the beginning of the book

b. the page on the reverse side of title page; it tells when the book was printed

c. additional information at the back of the book

d. list of some of the words used in the text with their meanings

e. list of sources the author used for research

f. first page; shows title, author, publisher

g. alphabetical list of names and ideas and the pages on which they can be found; appears at end of book

B. Circle a word or words to correctly complete each sentence.

1. The book's name appears on the (copyright page / title page).

2. The date of publication appears on the (copyright page / title page).

3. The (table of contents / index) lists the chapter titles.

4. To find information about Chief Sitting Bull in a U.S. history text, you would look in the (appendix / index).

5. To define the word *colony*, you could look in the (glossary / bibliography) of your history text.

6. Items in the (table of contents / index) are arranged in alphabetical order.

TEXTBOOKS: The First Few Pages

The *title page* is usually the first page in a textbook.

A. Study the sample title page. Then fill in the following blanks.

> **EXPLORING
> UNITED STATES HISTORY**
>
> Will Wilson & Bev Booth
>
> Masters Publishing Co.
> Buffalo, New York

1. Book title: _____

2. Author(s): _____

3. Publisher: _____

4. Place of publication: _____

The *copyright page* is usually the second page in the textbook. It is usually found on the reverse side of the title page.

B. Answer these questions about information found on a copyright page.

1. Find the word *copyright* in a dictionary. Write the definition here.

   _____

   _____

2. Why might it be important for a reader to know a textbook's copyright date?

   _____

C. Look at the copyright page of any book. Then fill in the following blanks.

1. Find the symbol that appears by the word *copyright*. Draw the symbol here. _____

2. What was the date of the most recent publication? _____

3. What person or company holds the copyright? _____

D. On the back of this sheet, create a title page for *Rock Climbing for Beginners* written by I. M. Slippin. The book was published by the Wilderness Book Company in Denver, Colorado.

TEXTBOOKS: Using the Table of Contents

The *table of contents* is an outline of the whole book. It tells what main ideas are covered. A textbook's table of contents often divides the book's subject matter into units. These units are then divided into chapters. The table of contents lists the page on which each chapter begins.

A. Write **T** or **F** to show whether each item is a **true** or **false** description of a table of contents. If you need help, turn to the table of contents of any textbook.

The table of contents:

1. ____ is usually the last page in the book.

2. ____ tells a reader how many chapters are in the book.

3. ____ defines words used in the book.

4. ____ tells on what page a chapter begins.

5. ____ lists items in alphabetical order.

6. ____ lists other books on the same subject.

7. ____ gives information about the author.

8. ____ lists items in the order they appear in the book.

9. ____ tells a reader what general subjects the book covers.

10. ____ breaks chapters down into smaller sections called units.

B. Circle the number of each item that would appear in a table of contents.

1. author's name
2. vocabulary words
3. page numbers
4. unit titles
5. publisher
6. chapter names
7. review questions
8. word meanings

C. On the back of this sheet, create a portion of the table of contents for a life science textbook. The first unit of the book begins on page 2 and is about plants. Chapters within that unit begin on pages 2, 4, 10, and 14. In this order, the chapters cover *seedlings, root systems, stems,* and *leaves.*

TEXTBOOKS: USING THE INDEX

At the back of most textbooks is an *index*. This section lists the important names and ideas found within the book. After each listing, the index tells the page numbers where the reader can find information about that subject. Index listings appear in alphabetical order.

A. Write **TOC** before the words and phrases that describe a **table of contents**. Write **I** before words and phrases that describe an **index**.

1. ____ usually in the front of the book

2. ____ usually at the end of the book

3. ____ an outline of *general* subjects covered in the book

4. ____ a long list of *specific* topics presented in the book

5. ____ arranged in alphabetical order

6. ____ arranged in order of appearance in the book

7. ____ may *not* list a specific person discussed in the book

8. ____ will *not* give chapter or unit titles

B. To use an index, readers need to know alphabetical order and the name or subject they want to find. Read the names and terms listed below. They all appear in a textbook called *A Nation Divided: The Civil War*. On the back of this sheet, rewrite the words and terms in alphabetical order.

NORTH VS. SOUTH

abolitionists	Confederacy
Grant, Ulysses S.	anti-slavery movement
Lee, Robert E.	Gettysburg, Battle of
Bull Run, Battle of	Lincoln, Abraham
women in the war	Davis, Jefferson
Reconstruction period	Barton, Clara

TEXTBOOKS: USING CHAPTER CLUES

Always *preview* a textbook chapter before you read it. First, go through a chapter from beginning to end, reading only the boldfaced *titles and heads.* Then look for important points emphasized by *charts, graphs, maps,* and *pictures.* Also notice *highlighted key words,* and read *end-of-chapter summaries.* Be sure to preview *questions before and after the chapter.* They indicate topics you should pay close attention to as you read.

A. Think about the information provided in the headings below. Then circle a letter to answer each question.

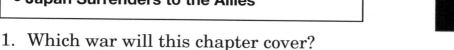

> **CHAPTER 14: THE SECOND WORLD WAR**
> - **Roosevelt Re-elected President**
> - **Pearl Harbor Attacked**
> - **War Begins**
> - **Japan Surrenders to the Allies**

1. Which war will this chapter cover?
   a. Revolutionary War   b. World War II   c. Civil War

2. Who was president at the outset of the war?
   a. Roosevelt   b. Lincoln   c. can't tell from headings

3. Who won the first battle of the war?
   a. Japan   b. the Allies   c. can't tell from headings

4. What part of the Second World War will be covered in this chapter?
   a. European battles   b. only Pacific battles   c. can't tell from headings

5. Who won the War?
   a. the Allies   b. Japan   c. can't tell from headings

B. Use any textbook for this activity. Circle the chapter clues it provides.

chapter title

charts, maps, and/or graphs

end-of-chapter summary

end-of-chapter questions

boldfaced headings

boldfaced or highlighted key words

questions before the chapter

C. On the back of this sheet, list any other chapter clues your textbook provides.

TEXTBOOKS: The Glossary

The *glossary* of a textbook is like a little dictionary. It lists, in alphabetical order, words that readers may find unfamiliar. It gives the meaning of each word only as it is used within the text. The glossary is usually near the end of the book.

A. Circle a letter to show which words correctly complete each sentence.

    1. Glossary words are listed in the order

        a. of the alphabet.   b. in which they appear in the book.

    2. A glossary gives

        a. all possible meanings of a word.

        b. the meaning for the word as it is used in the book.

    3. You can usually find the glossary

        a. near the front of the book.

        b. near the end of the book.

B. Read this passage from a world geography textbook. Write the six boldfaced words in alphabetical order on the lines.

Volcanoes of Indonesia

Indonesia is dotted with **volcanoes**. Java and Baliare are the most **volcanically active** islands in the world. Over 155 volcanoes are active and could **erupt** at any time.

Although volcanoes can be destructive, they also help the people of Indonesia. **Fertile** volcanic soil means rich farmlands. Rocks near volcanoes often contain valuable ores and minerals, and much of Indonesia is rich in gold, silver, copper, and **sulfur**. Volcanoes can produce **geothermal** energy when their heat turns underground water to steam.

_____   _____   _____

_____   _____   _____

C. On the back of this sheet, create a glossary that lists the words you alphabetized in *Part B*. A dictionary can help you write definitions. Be sure to choose the meaning of the word as it is used in the passage.

UNDERSTANDING YOUR TEXTBOOK: A PUZZLE

To complete the puzzle, match the words in the box to the clues.

ACROSS

4. This first textbook page tells the names of the author and publisher.

5. Items in the index are arranged according to the ____.

8. This chapter-by-chapter outline of topics appears early in the book.

10. An ____ near the end of the text may give added information.

DOWN

1. The ____ lists sources the author used for research.

2. This claims the legal right to publish the material.

3. These may appear before and/or after each chapter. Their answers contain key information.

6. This list defines new or unusual words that appear in the book.

7. The ____ lists specific names and ideas and the pages on which they can be found.

9. This is one of the main parts into which a textbook is divided.

alphabet
appendix
bibliography
chapter
copyright
glossary
index
questions
table of contents
title page

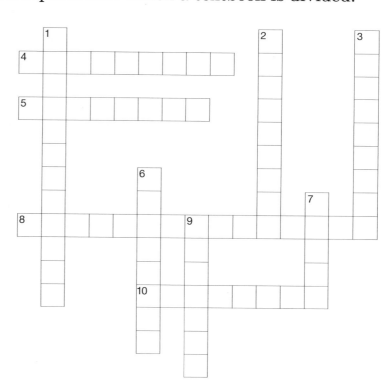

SKIMMING AND SCANNING

The **way** you read often depends on two things—your purpose for reading and the kind of reading material involved. Three reading methods, *skimming, scanning,* and *detailed reading,* are described below.

SKIMMING: reading for an overview of the material. To skim a paragraph, read the title and the topic sentence (usually the first sentence). If the first sentence doesn't tell what the paragraph is about, try the last one.

SCANNING: glancing through written material until you find a particular piece of information. For example, to find a phone number, scan the phone book page until you see a certain name. Scanning is usually the fastest reading method.

DETAILED READING: reading material word-for-word from beginning to end, noting details that support the main idea.

A. Draw a line to match each reading **method** on the left with a reading **purpose** on the right.

1. skimming

2. scanning

3. detailed reading

a. find the date of the Battle of Bunker Hill in an article on the American Revolution

b. enjoy a mystery novel

c. quickly decide what a magazine article called "The Crash" is about

B. *Skim* the following paragraph. On the line, write the main idea.

THE ANGEL OF THE BATTLEFIELD

Civil War nurse Clara Barton spent most of her life helping others. She risked her own safety to take care of wounded soldiers and carry supplies into battle. When the war ended, Barton continued to help those in need. She formed a group to search for missing men and, in 1881, founded the American Red Cross.

MAIN IDEA: _____

C. *Scan* the paragraph in *Part B* to find the year Clara Barton founded the American Red Cross. Write the year on the line. _____

MORE SKIMMING PRACTICE

When you *skim* written material, you read for a quick overview.

A. Skim the paragraph. *Read* and *circle* the title. *Read* and *underline* the first sentence. *Write* the paragraph's main idea on the line.

THE SPONGE

The sponge is one of the simplest living creatures. It doesn't move about like most animals but lives attached to rocks. Its body is like an empty sack full of holes. A sponge does not have a mouth. It eats by pulling water filled with tiny animals through the holes in its body.

MAIN IDEA: _____

B. Skim the article. *Read* and *circle* the title and subheadings. *Read* and *underline* all topic sentences. On the back of this sheet, *write*, in your own words, three main ideas that the article presents.

THE SINKING OF THE TITANIC

Her builders believed that she was unsinkable. But on her maiden voyage the steamship *Titanic* went down. Some 1,517 passengers and crewmembers lost their lives in one of the greatest tragedies in the history of the sea.

A Floating Palace

The *Titanic* was a wonder of her era. She was the largest, fastest vessel of her time. With a grand staircase and a saltwater swimming pool, the luxury liner cost $10 million and took three years to build.

Bigshots on Board

On April 10, 1912, the *Titanic* carried many well-known passengers out of England. Among those headed to New York was Bruce Ismay, head of the steamship line. Also on board were Colonel John J. Astor and his bride. Astor was one of the richest men in America.

The Deadly Crash

After four days at sea, the *Titanic* hit an iceberg. The crash tore a 300-foot gash in the ship's hull. Less than three hours later, the ship vanished into the Atlantic.

SCANNING PRACTICE

TODAY'S WEATHER
PARTLY CLOUDY
SCATTERED SHOWERS
HIGH **62**, LOW **46**

You *scan* written material when you are looking for a certain piece of information.

Scan each item to find the answer to the question. Write the answer on the line.

1. What is Joe Perez's phone number? _____

> Pera, Richard
>   812 S. W. 15th Ave. 221-6970
> Perez, Joe
>   4639 N.E. Oak St. 690-4432
> Perfect Image Beauty Salon
>   222 W. Main St. 222-6115
> Perkins, Alice and Pete
>   4192 S. W. Tulip Ter. 891-9962

2. What was the day's hightemperature? _____

3. What program is on Channel 5 at 5:00 p.m.? _____

CH	3:00	3:30	4:00	4:30	5:00
2	NBA Basketball	NBA Basketball	NBA Basketball	NBA Basketball	Early News
5	All My Problems	All My Problems	Talking with Sue	Talking with Sue	Sports Chat
15	Business Hour	Business Hour	Rock's Videos	Rock's Videos	World News

4. When was Thomas Edison born? _____

> **Edison, Thomas Alva** (1847–1931), may have been the world's greatest inventor. His electric lightbulb, phonograph, and motion picture machine greatly changed the way people lived. Edison was born in Milan, Ohio. When he entered public school, some teachers complained that he was not very smart. Instead of paying attention in class, Edison was thinking about things he had seen and read on his own.

5. What was the price of a postage stamp in 1910? _____

> ### U.S.A. STATISTICS—1910
>
> Population.................91.9 million   Price of a postage stamp....$.05
> Number of states 46   Price of an automobile........$1,750.00
>   Average monthly salary for teachers............ $62.23

THE LIBRARY: WORDS TO KNOW

There are three types of *libraries:* public libraries, school libraries, and special libraries (such as law or science libraries). Public and school libraries have both *fiction* and *nonfiction* books available for borrowing. Most also have materials like magazines, videos, and tapes.

A. The 10 terms below are important to know when you use a library. Write a letter to match each term on the left with its definition on the right.

1. _____ **fiction**

2. _____ **nonfiction**

3. _____ **biography**

4. _____ **reference book**

5. _____ **online catalog**

6. _____ **Dewey decimal system**

7. _____ **periodical**

8. _____ **bar code**

9. _____ **librarian**

10. _____ **media center**

a. a numbered method of arranging nonfiction

b. a person who works in the library

c. computers containing information on all the books in the library

d. a set of vertical bars put on library materials; allows a scanner to check out and keep track of them

e. an account of a person's life written by someone else

f. a story based on imaginary people and happenings

g. a written work based on facts

h. a book of organized information that can be used to find facts

i. a library that contains magazines, tapes, and videos

j. a magazine put out each week, month, and so on

B. Circle the word in each group that does **not** belong. On the back of the sheet, explain why that item does not belong.

1. librarian   author   reference book

2. media center   periodical   library

3. fiction   biography   nonfiction   bar code

4. reference book   nonfiction   fiction   biography

THE LIBRARY: FICTION AND NONFICTION

Most school and public libraries arrange books under the categories of *fiction* or *nonfiction*. Most fiction and nonfiction books are circulating materials. You can check them out and take them home. Some materials, especially nonfiction, are *non-circulating.* You may only use them in the library. Many reference books and magazines are non-circulating materials.

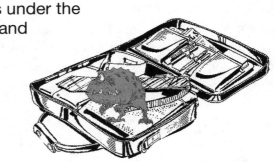

A. Read the book titles below. Write **F** if you think the book is **fiction**. Write **NF** if you think the book is **nonfiction**.

1. ____ *There's a Monster in My Suitcase*

2. ____ *The Life of President George Washington*

3. ____ *First Aid for Hikers*

4. ____ *The Mystery of Huntington's Hill*

5. ____ *Spanish for Beginners*

Fiction books are arranged *alphabetically* by the *author's last name.* For example, look under the letter *L* for a book written by Jack London.

B. Renumber the following fiction books in the order they would appear on the library shelves. The first has been identified for you.

____ 1. *The Adventures of Tom Sawyer* by Mark Twain

_1_ 2. *The Chocolate War* by Robert Cormier

____ 3. *The Haunting of Hill House* by Shirley Jackson

____ 4. *The Pigman* by Paul Zindel

____ 5. *The Outsiders* by S.E. Hinton

C. Many libraries organize nonfiction books according to the *Dewey decimal system.* This system uses numbers to identify 10 major subject categories. Draw a line to match each title on the left with a subject category on the right.

1. *The Spanish-American War*   a. Technology

2. *Industrial Robots*   b. Religion

3. *Jewish Festivals and Holidays*   c. History

THE LIBRARY: THE DEWEY DECIMAL SYSTEM

Most libraries arrange nonfiction books according to the *Dewey* decimal system. The numbers 000 to 999 are used to divide books into ten subject categories.

DEWEY DECIMAL CLASSIFICATIONS			
000–099	General Works	500–599	Science
100–199	Philosophy	600–699	Technology (applied science)
200–299	Religion	700–799	Fine Arts (art, music, sports, hobbies)
300–399	Social Sciences	800–899	Literature
400–499	Languages	900–999	History

You do not need to memorize this system. Libraries post the information.

A. Read the list of topics. Write the numbers and category for each book. The first one has been done for you.

1. famous operas

   700–799, Fine Arts

2. World War II

3. French grammar

4. the Internet

B. Some titles do not clearly indicate the subject of the book. Read the book title and its Dewey number. Then circle the letter of the correct subject for each title.

1. *Grab Your Umbrella* (551)
   a. collection of humorous poems
   b. book about forecasting weather
   c. guide to rainy-day activities

2. *The Story of Joseph* (970.1)
   a. Bible story
   b. book about Native American Chief Joseph
   c. story of medical scientist Joseph Lister

C. Each major Dewey decimal category is divided into subtopics. For example, within Science (500–599), books on astronomy have numbers in the 520s. A book on stars is numbered 523.8. On the back of this sheet, list these books in the order you would find them on the shelves.

793.8 *Astounding Magic Tricks*

598.9 *Big Birds of Prey*

551.6 *Forecasting Tomorrow's Weather*

769.5 *The Stamp Collector's Handbook*

THE LIBRARY: Call Numbers

The library prints a *call number* on the spine of each book. The call number for a *fiction* book has two parts. The first line has the letters *FIC* for fiction (or *J* for juvenile fiction). The second line has the author's last name or first three letters of the last name. The call number for a *nonfiction* book includes a Dewey decimal number and the first three letters of the author's last name. (See examples below.)

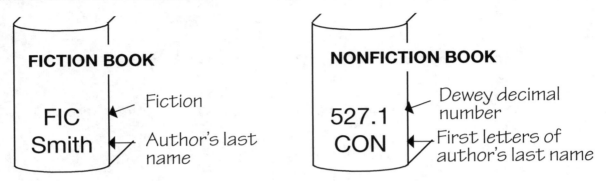

A. Circle a word or words to correctly complete each sentence.

1. The call number is located on the (title page / spine) of a book.

2. The call numbers of (juvenile fiction / journalism) books begin with *J*.

3. The second line of a call number identifies the (title / author).

4. Nonfiction call numbers start with a (title / Dewey decimal number).

5. The call number letters FIC show that a book is (fiction / factual).

B. Rewrite the call numbers on the blanks at the bottom of the spines to show the order in which the books would be shelved. *Note:* Books with the same Dewey decimal numbers are arranged alphabetically by the first three letters of the author's last name.

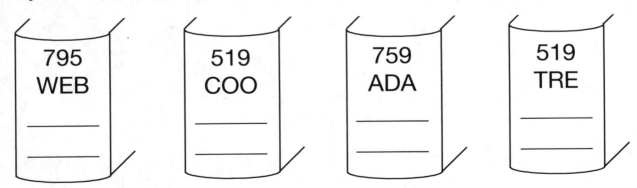

C. On the back of this sheet, write the call number for each book shown in *Part B*. Next to each call number, name the category to which the book belongs.

THE LIBRARY: Using the Card Catalog

The *card catalog* helps you identify call numbers so you can find books in the library. In many libraries, the card catalog is being replaced by an online catalog. In a card catalog, cards are alphabetically arranged in a cabinet with many drawers. There are three cards for each book: an *author card,* a *title card,* and a subject card. Look at these sample cards:

SUBJECT CARD

```
        Solar Heat

921.7 Wong, Dennis
        Heat from the Heavens
        illustrated by Kate Harper
        New York: Hometown Press, 1996
        123 p.: col. illus and index
```

TITLE CARD

```
        Heat from the Heavens

921.7 Wong, Dennis
        illustrated by Kate Harper
        New York: Hometown Press, 1996
        123 p.: col. illus and index

        1. solar heat  2. energy, solar
```

AUTHOR CARD

```
        Wong, Dennis

921.7 Heat from the Heavens
        illustrated by Kate Harper
        New York: Hometown Press, 1996
        123 p.: col. illus and index

        1. solar heat  2. energy, solar
```

A. Which type of card would you look for to locate the following items? Write **title, author,** or **subject**. Then write the letter you would look under. The first one has been done for you.

1. a book written by Edgar Allan Poe   *author*   P

2. the story of the first Thanksgiving   _____ ____

3. an auto repair manual   _____ ____

4. a fiction book called *Hidden Bay*   _____ ____

5. a nonfiction book called *A Visitor's Guide to Maine*   _____ ____

B. Select one of the sample cards above and use it to answer these questions. Write your answers on the back of this sheet.

1. What is the title?

2. Who is the author?

3. What is the subject of the book?

4. What is the call number?

5. How many pages are in the book?

6. Is this book fiction or nonfiction? How do you know?

THE COMPUTERIZED CATALOG

Today, libraries use a *computerized catalog* to keep track of materials. Like the card catalog, the computerized catalog can help you locate materials on the shelves. The information on the computer screen also reports book availability (how many copies are checked in or out, current due dates, and which library *branches* have copies). It allows you to reserve the next available copy by putting a hold on the material.

MENU
1. **Title**
2. **Author**
3. **Subject**

The *menu* allows the user to find a book by its title, author, or subject.

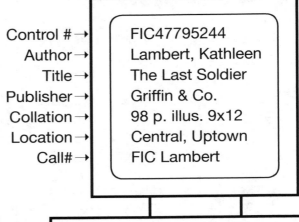

Control # → FIC47795244
Author → Lambert, Kathleen
Title → The Last Soldier
Publisher → Griffin & Co.
Collation → 98 p. illus. 9x12
Location → Central, Uptown
Call# → FIC Lambert

The screen shows the same information found on a card in the card catalog. . . and more.

To complete the puzzle, use the information above and the clues below.

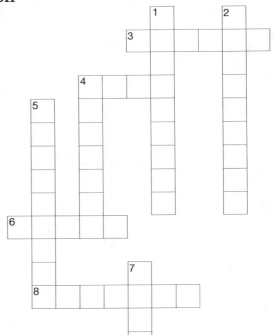

ACROSS

3. *K. Lambert* is an ____.
4. *FIC Lambert* is a ____ number.
6. *The Last Soldier* is a ____.
8. The menu allows you to search by title, author, or ____.

DOWN

1. *Griffin & Co.* is a ____.
2. *number of pages* and *book size* are called ____.
4. *FIC47795244* is a ____ number.
5. *Central* and *Uptown* are two ____ , or branches of the library.
7. The ____ shows three ways to find a book.

THE LIBRARY: Skills Review

Mastering library skills can help you study more effectively.

A. Use words from the box to fill in the blanks.

branch	subject	computerized catalog
menu	titles	Dewey decimal number

Kevin entered the main (1)_____ of the city library. He needed information on the rain forests of South America. Kevin's first stop was at the library's (2)_____ . When he tapped the keyboard, a (3)_____ appeared on the screen. It asked him to choose author, title, or subject. Kevin selected (4)_____. Then he typed rain forests. Again the screen gave Kevin choices. He picked Rain Forests, South American. After Kevin made his selection, the screen showed the (5)_____ of several books about South American rain forests. Kevin clicked on one of those books and got information he needed to find it on the shelf. When he saw that the (6)_____ was 564.8, he knew he could find more books on rain forests in that part of the library, too.

B. Circle the hidden words in the puzzle. They may go up, down, across, backward, or diagonally. Check off each word as you find it.

_____ AUTHOR

_____ BIOGRAPHY

_____ CALL NUMBER

_____ CARD CATALOG

_____ CIRCULATING

_____ FICTION

_____ JUVENILE

_____ LIBRARIAN

```
W C B I O G R A P H Y T K A
D O A C M F I C T I O N A P
U P U R P I E G O M Z L R J
H O T P D L I B R A R I A N
P I H X G C U L C P A L E D
S E O A N E A J Z D O C G I
C I R C U L A T I N G O H N
N I E C D T O G A M V L K A
S N M J U V E N I L E R O Y
S E V O S E J K E A O N E H
C A L L N U M B E R E G M A
```

REFERENCE: INFORMATION RESOURCES

Reference books are rich gold mines of information! Usually, reference materials are shelved together in one part of the library. Most often, they must be used in the library and cannot be checked out.

A. The following reference works can be helpful when you are writing a report or need a question answered. Write a letter to match each reference book on the left with its description on the right.

1. ____ **dictionary**

2. ____ **encyclopedia**

3. ____ **atlas**

4. ____ **thesaurus**

5. ____ ***Readers' Guide to Periodical Literature***

6. ____ **almanac**

7. ____ **quotation book**

8. ____ **biographical reference**

a. published yearly, it gives current facts and statistics on many subjects

b. contains maps, charts, and facts about places

c. a book of synonyms

d. contains information about famous people

e. a collection of famous sayings

f. an alphabetical collection of words and their definitions

g. a set of books containing alphabetized entries on almost any subject

h. an alphabetically arranged index that lists current magazine articles

B. Which reference book could help you answer each question? Write the name of the reference book on the line.

1. What does the word *cogitate* mean? _____

2. In what state is the Columbia River? _____

3. In what year was Steven Spielberg born? _____

4. What recent magazines contain information about airline safety? _____

C. Use reference books to find the answers to any two of the questions in *Part B.* Write the answers on the back of this sheet.

Study Skills 1 • © Saddleback Educational Publishing • www.sdlback.com

REFERENCE: ALPHABETICAL ORDER

Information in many reference books is arranged in *alphabetical order.* Strong alphabetizing skills can help you quickly find information in a dictionary, thesaurus, or encyclopedia. Follow the instructions below to sharpen your skills.

A. Supply the missing letter in each group. The first one has been done for you.

1. a _b_ c   3. f ___ h   5. q ___ s   7. w ___ y   9. c ___ e
2. j ___ l   4. m ___ o   6. l ___ n   8. r ___ t   10. b ___ d

B. Rewrite each group of letters in alphabetical order. The first one has been done for you.

1. u t w v x   _t u v w x_   4. j k i m l   _____
2. z x y w v   _____   5. e d f h g   _____
3. s q p r t   _____   6. c e a d b   _____

C. Number the words in each list in alphabetical order. In list 1, use the first letter of each word to determine the order. In list 2, look at the second letter. In list 3, look at the third letter of each word.

1. ___ gentle   2. ___ traffic   3. ___ pleasure
   ___ elephant   ___ temper   ___ plastic
   ___ arrival   ___ taste   ___ plump
   ___ fawn   ___ tone   ___ plow
   ___ beautiful   ___ tick   ___ plight

D. Form a sentence by writing the words in each group in alphabetical order. The first one has been done for you. Then, on the back of this sheet, write an "alphabetical order" sentence of your own.

1. die cats early bad all. _____ *All bad cats die early.* _____

2. tomatoes only McDonald ripe farmer picks.

   _____

3. fresh Bob near bought Newark fruit.

   _____

4. the motored merry water many near motorcyclists.

   _____

MORE ALPHABETIZING PRACTICE

Knowing how to put words in alphabetical order will help you quickly find information in reference books.

A. Circle the word in each group that would come *first* in a reference book.

1. bowling   bird   Brazil

2. medicine   mineral   mural

3. Greece   golf   gold

4. ruby   radish   railroad

B. Reference books list people according to their *last name*. Write the following famous names in alphabetical order. (*Hint*: People with the same last names will be placed in alphabetical order by their *first names*.)

Booker T. Washington	**Marilyn Monroe**	**Amelia Earhart**
Sandra Day O'Connor	**Albert Einstein**	**Babe Ruth**
George Washington	**Cesar Chavez**	**Henry Ford**
Louis Armstrong	**Gerald Ford**	**Elvis Presley**

1. _____

2. _____

3. _____

4. _____

5. _____

6. _____

7. _____

8. _____

9. _____

10. _____

11. _____

12. _____

C. You can find all these topics in the **P** volume of an encyclopedia. Write the topics in alphabetical order.

pyramid	**Poland**	**Thomas Paine**	**Pacific Ocean**

1. _____

2. _____

3. _____

4. _____

D. These words all appear on the same page of a dictionary. On the back of this sheet, write the words in alphabetical order.

grape	**grandparent**	**granny**	**granola**	**grandchild**

REFERENCE: DICTIONARY GUIDE WORDS

Have you ever noticed the two *guide* words at the top of each dictionary page? These words help you quickly find a word and its definition. The guide word on the left is the first word listed on the page. The guide word on the right is the last word listed on that page.

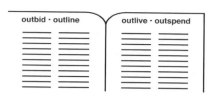

A. The word *cloud,* for example, would appear on a page with the guide words **closet** and **clown**. Suppose a dictionary page is headed by the guide words **hunk** and **husky**. Circle the words you could find on that page.

hurdle	husband	hutch	hurry
hunter	husk	hyacinth	hurricane
handsome	heal	hydrogen	hunger

B. Write a letter to match each word on the left with the guide words it would fall between.

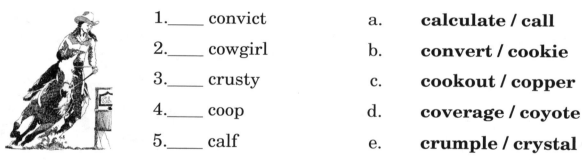

1._____ convict   a.   **calculate / call**

2._____ cowgirl   b.   **convert / cookie**

3._____ crusty   c.   **cookout / copper**

4._____ coop   d.   **coverage / coyote**

5._____ calf   e.   **crumple / crystal**

C. Imagine a dictionary page with the guide words **Grand Canyon** and **grapefruit**. Decide whether each word below would come *on, before,* or *after* this page. Write **on, before,** or **after** on the line.

1. _____ granite   4. _____ great   7. _____ graveyard

2. _____ green   5. _____ grammar   8. _____ grape

3. _____ grant   6. _____ grapevine   9. _____ gorilla

D. Locate the following words in a dictionary. What *guide words* head the page on which you find each word? Write them on the back of this sheet.

mackintosh	catnip	rodeo
dumbwaiter	screech	afghan

REFERENCE: Dictionary Definitions

A dictionary lists all the different *definitions* of a given word. In addition to the word's meaning, the dictionary provides other information about the word and how to use it. An entry for the word *grease* is shown below. Some of the main parts of the entry are pointed out below.

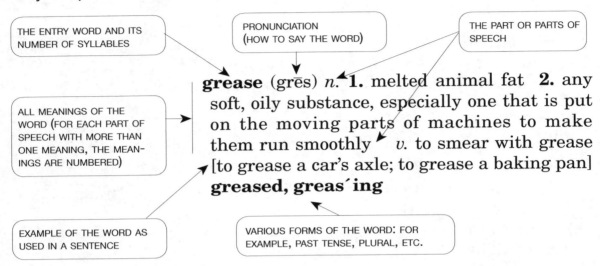

A. Use the dictionary entry above to find the meaning of *grease* as it is used in each sentence. Write the definition on the line below the sentence.

1. That rusty gate will open more easily if you *grease* its hinges.

_____

2. The cook kept a jar of bacon *grease* in his kitchen.

_____

3. A squirt of *grease* will fix a squeaky bicycle wheel.

_____

B. On the lines below, write two original sentences. In the first, use *grease* as a noun. In the second, use *grease* as a verb.

1. _____

_____

2. _____

_____

C. Look up the word *brass* in a dictionary. How many definitions does your dictionary list? Number and write the definitions on the back of this sheet.

   Study Skills 1 • © Saddleback Educational Publishing • www.sdlback.com

REFERENCE: A DICTIONARY TELLS PARTS OF SPEECH

The dictionary usually shows a word's part of *speech* in italic type. The part of speech is listed before the definition and is abbreviated as follows:

n. - noun	**adv.** - adverb	**pron.** - pronoun	**interj.** - interjection
v. - verb	**adj.** - adjective	**conj.** - conjunction	**prep.** - preposition

When a word can be used in more than one way, the dictionary will show more than one part of speech.

EXAMPLE: raid (rād) n. **1.** a sudden attack **2.** the act of entering a place to arrest people who are breaking the law v. to make a raid on [to *raid* a town]

A. Find each of these words in a dictionary. Write the abbreviations for **all** parts of speech listed for each word. The first one has been done for you.

1. radio __n., v.__

2. malt _____

3. crop _____

4. blunt _____

5. bodily _____

6. gum _____

7. lost _____

8. lower _____

9. nose _____

10. rebel _____

B. Notice how the boldfaced word is used in each sentence below. Then circle the letter that identifies the *part of speech*. Use a dictionary if you need help.

1. They began the long **climb** around 5:00 A.M.

   a. noun   b. verb   c. adjective

2. Walter will quickly **climb** the ladder of success.

   a. noun   b. verb   c. adjective

3. We wanted to swim in the **calm**, cool water.

   a. noun   b. verb   c. adjective

4. The babysitter tried to **calm** the rowdy children.

   a. noun   b. verb   c. adjective

5. This moment of sunshine may be the **calm** before the storm!

   a. noun   b. verb   c. adjective

C. On the back of this sheet, write two sentences using the same word. In one sentence use the word as a noun. In the other, use the word as a verb.

REFERENCE: More Dictionary Information

A dictionary entry shows how a word divides into *syllables*. The divisions are usually shown by small dots. You can use this information to decide how to divide a word at the end of a written line.

EXAMPLE: hi•ber•nate

A. Rewrite each word. Place a dot between each syllable. Remember that a one-syllable word is not divided. Use a dictionary for help.

1. sensation _____   4. odor _____

2. sight _____   5. vibrate _____

3. hearing _____   6. tasteless _____

The dictionary uses dots, dashes, and other signs to show how to pronounce a word. These signs are called diacritical marks. A pronunciation guide that explains the meaning of the signs is generally found at the front.

PRONUNCIATION GUIDE				
ă bat	ō go	û fur	ə =	a in ago
ā ape	ô fall, for	ch chin		e in agent
ä cot, car	o͝o book	sh she		i in pencil
ĕ ten	o͞o school	th thin		o in atom
ē me	oi soil	th then		u in circus
ĭ fit	ou out	zh treasure		
ī ice	ŭ up	ŋ sing		

B. Look at the sample pronunciation guide above. Show how to pronounce each word by writing it with syllable divisions and **diacritical marks.** Put an accent mark(´) after the syllable that should be stressed. (No accent mark is needed for one-syllable words.) Use a dictionary for help.

1. meat _____   4. mostly _____

2. moldy _____   5. snake _____

3. win _____   6. chimney _____

C. Use the dictionary pronunciation key to decode the following quote from the humorous writer, James Thurber. On the back of the sheet, write the correct spelling of the words.

> Ĭf ī kôld thə rôŋ nŭm′bər, wŭt did yo͞o an′sər fôr?

DICTIONARY REVIEW

Understanding all the parts of a dictionary entry can help you write and pronounce words correctly.

A. Choose words from the box to identify the circled parts of the dictionary entry. Write the letter of each choice on a line. The first one has been done for you.

> **(a) main entry word**
> **(b) part of speech**
> **(c) usage example**
> **(d) pronunciation**
> **(e) definition**

1. _a_   2. ____

crook (krŏŏk) *n.* **1.** A thing or part that is bent or curved [a crook in the road] **2.** a shepherd's staff with a hook at the end **3.** a person who steals or cheats *v.* to bend or curve [to crook one's arm]

3. ____   4. ____

5. ____   6. ____

mis take (mi stāk´) *n.* an idea, answer, act, etc. that is wrong; an error *v.* **1.** to get a wrong idea; misunderstand **2.** to think that a certain thing is something else [It is easy to *mistake* one twin for another.]

7. ____   8. ____

B. Use a dictionary to find a word that fits each of the following descriptions. On the back of this sheet, write a sentence using each word. Underline the example word.

1. a word with three syllables

2. a word with an accented first syllable

3. a word that can be used as a noun or a verb

4. a word with a *long e* sound (ē)

REFERENCE: THE ENCYCLOPEDIA

An *encyclopedia* gives information in essay form. A *general encyclopedia* tells about persons, places, events, and things in every field. A *specialized encyclopedia* has topics from just one field, such as art. A general encyclopedia can be a good place to begin your research. Most libraries have **many** encyclopedias. Be sure to find one that is easy for you to read and understand. You may also find encyclopedias online.

Most encyclopedias are sets of books or *volumes*. The volumes and the topics in each one are arranged in alphabetical order. *Guide words* at the top of each page can help you locate topics. There may be an *index* at the back of each volume or one complete index in a separate volume.

A. Reread the information above. Then write **T** or **F** to show whether each statement is **true** or **false**.

1. _____ A general encyclopedia tells about most subjects.

2. _____ Famous people *are not* listed in general encyclopedias.

3. _____ Most general encyclopedias have several volumes.

4. _____ Encyclopedia volumes are arranged in alphabetical order.

5. _____ Encyclopedias list events in the order they happened.

6. _____ You can't find a topic without using an encyclopedia index.

B. Read the list of topics below. Which of the 10 volumes would give information on each topic? Write the volume number next to the topic.

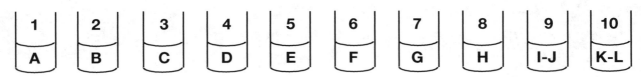

1	2	3	4	5	6	7	8	9	10
A	B	C	D	E	F	G	H	I-J	K-L

1. _____ Halloween   4. _____ Thomas Jefferson

2. _____ Japan   5. _____ lightning

3. _____ basketball   6. _____ dragon

C. The word *encyclopedia* comes from Greek words meaning "well-rounded education." On the back of this sheet, explain why *encyclopedia* is a fitting name for these important reference books.

REFERENCE: THE WORLD ATLAS

A *world atlas* is a book full of maps and facts about most places on earth.

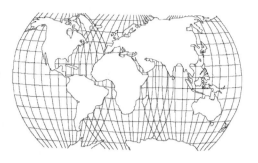

A. The atlas *table of contents* lists all the maps, charts, and tables and their page numbers. Look at this small section of a table of contents. Put a check (✓) by questions you could answer by turning to pages listed.

TABLE OF CONTENTS

Western Hemisphere
pages 61 through 125

North America 61   Mexico 63
Central America 62   West Indies......... 64
Caribbean Islands.... 65   South America ... 65

Geographical Facts and Figures
pages 142 through 200

Principal Mountains of the World 142
Great Oceans and Seas of the World... 143
Principal Rivers of the World 144

1. ____ What country borders Mexico to the north?

2. ____ What is the highest mountain in the world?

3. ____ In what year did the California gold rush begin?

4. ____ Who is the U.S. ambassador to Brazil?

5. ____ Which South American country is the farthest north—Peru, Brazil, or Venezuela?

B. The *index* lists specific place names and page numbers. Many indexes list guide letters and numbers to help locate places on a map. Look at the index section. Then answer the questions.

INDEX		GUIDE LETTER & NUMBER
NAME	PAGE	
Portland, Maine	46	...........E2
Portland, Ore.	32	............B4
Portland, Tenn.	41	...........A5
Portland, Texas........	50	............F4

1. A map on what page shows the location of Portland, Maine? _____

2. What is the guide letter and number of Portland, Oregon? _____

3. Which *does not* have a Portland:
Texas, Kansas, or Tennessee? _____

C. Find the entry for your city or town in an atlas index. On the back of this sheet, write the page number listed in the index. If the index lists them, also write the guide letter and number.

REFERENCE: THE THESAURUS

A *thesaurus* lists *synonyms*—words that have nearly the same meaning. When you write, a thesaurus can help you find interesting words and avoid repeating overused ones. Entry words in a thesaurus are alphabetized, just as they are in a dictionary. Study the sample entries below.

ugly, *adj.* hideous, repulsive, forbidding
umbrella, *n.* parasol, bumbershoot, sunshade
unafraid, *adj.* undaunted, courageous, brave, daring
upset, *v.* bother, perturb, disturb, unsettle
　　　n. defeat *adj.* uneasy, disturbed, bothered

A. Replace each boldfaced word by writing a synonym on the line. Use the entries above for suggestions.

　1. It was an **ugly** (_____) day with dark clouds hanging low in the sky.

　2. Sadly, I had left my **umbrella** (_____) at home.

　3. I became more **upset** (_____) as big raindrops began to fall.

　4. "I'll be **unafraid** (_____) and face the storm!" I exclaimed.

B. Circle a letter to show which words correctly complete each sentence.

　1. A thesaurus can help you

　　a. find synonyms for words.
　　b. divide words into syllables.

　2. A thesaurus is organized much like

　　a. an atlas.
　　b. a dictionary.

　3. Entry words are listed in

　　a. the table of contents.
　　b. alphabetical order.

　4. Each entry gives a word's

　　a. part of speech.
　　b. pronunciation.

C. Using a thesaurus for synonyms, write new job titles for these people on the back of this sheet. The first one has been done for you.

　1. door-to-door salesperson
　　　portal-to-portal peddler

　2. fire fighter

　3. window washer

　4. college student

　5. movie actor

REFERENCE: THE READERS' GUIDE TO PERIODICAL LITERATURE

A *periodical* is a magazine or newspaper that is published at regular intervals—usually daily, weekly, or monthly. The *Readers' Guide to Periodical Literature* can help you find specific articles in major periodicals. This library resource lists articles alphabetically by author and by subject.

Suppose you are researching a report on the Philippine Islands. If you looked in a *Readers' Guide* under "Philippines," you might see a listing like this:

The Philippines: Islands of Unrest. T. Newcomb. World News Today. 14:29–32 July 07

| TITLE OF ARTICLE | AUTHOR | MAGAZINE | VOLUME | PAGES | DATE |

A. Use the *Readers' Guide* entry above to answer these questions.

1. On what pages of the magazine will you find the article? _____

2. What is the date of the magazine issue? _____

3. What is the name of the magazine article?
   _____

4. Who wrote the article? _____

5. In what magazine will you find the article?
   _____

B. **Current** magazines are usually on the library shelves. To use a **back issue**, you may need to give the librarian a *periodical request slip.* Fill out this request slip as if you wanted the magazine listed in this *Readers' Guide* entry.

> Conquering the Common Cold. Dr. R. Graham. Modern Medicine. 31:104 Feb. 12 07

> **PERIODICAL REQUEST SLIP**
>
> NAME OF MAGAZINE: _____
>
> DATE OF ISSUE: month_____ day_____ year_____
>
> VOLUME _____   YOUR NAME _____

C. Go to the library. Find a current volume of the *Readers' Guide to Periodical Literature*. Look up the following three items. Write the information on the back of this sheet.

1. the title of a magazine article about golf star Tiger Woods
2. the name and volume number of a magazine with an article on the Ebola virus
3. the author of an article about infant car seats

REFERENCE: Almanacs

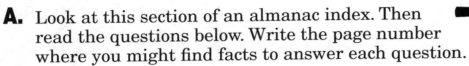

Almanacs are published once each year. They are a good place to find information quickly. These handy reference books summarize and report events, facts, and statistics of recent years. Almanacs include information on government, sports, economics, population, the weather, and so on.

A. Look at this section of an almanac index. Then read the questions below. Write the page number where you might find facts to answer each question.

Hockey, Ice		Holidays	
teams	417	Federal	196
All Star-team (2006)	356	Legal, public (U.S.)	196
NCAA champions	357	Flag display	197
National Hockey League	342–344	Religious	628–629
Olympic records	345	**Homes**	
Scoring leaders, all-time	346	Single-family, prices	614
Smythe Trophy	340	**Hong Kong**	525
Stanley Cup	351	Population	523
Hogs (on farms, prices)	140	Trade, U.S.	224

PAGE

_____ 1. What US holiday falls on Saturday, November 11?

_____ 2. In 2006, what was the average price of a house in Boston, Mass.?

_____ 3. What team won the last NCAA ice hockey championship?

_____ 4. According to the last census, how many people live in Hong Kong?

_____ 5. On which holidays is it correct to display the U.S. flag?

B. Put a check (✔) if you could use an almanac to answer the question.

1. _____ What baseball team won the 2005 World Series?

2. _____ What recent magazine contains an article on surfing?

3. _____ Which Arizona city is farthest south, Phoenix or Tucson?

4. _____ What is the legal driving age in Mississippi?

5. _____ How did the discovery of electricity change life in America?

6. _____ What is the tallest building in the United States?

C. Look at the questions you checked in *Part B*. Find the answer to each question. Write the topics on the back of this sheet.

REFERENCE: Biographical Dictionaries

A *biographical dictionary* contains alphabetized entries with information about the lives of famous people. Many of these dictionaries include people in a specific group, such as actors, authors, or U.S. presidents.

A. Draw a line to match each famous person on the left with a specialized biographical dictionary on the right.

1. Felix Salten
   (wrote *Bambi*)

2. Jonas Salk
   (discovered cure for polio)

3. Willie Mays
   (baseball star)

4. Herbert Hoover
   (U.S. President)

5. Bill Gates
   (Co-founder of Microsoft)

a. *Who's Who in American Sports*

b. *Junior Book of Authors*

c. *Dictionary of U.S. Presidents*

d. *Who's Who in America*

e. *20th Century Scientists*

B. Each item below lists three people who achieved fame in the same field. Unscramble the letters to name that field. Use a biographical dictionary or an encyclopedia for help.

1. Georgia O'Keeffe, Pablo Picasso, Claude Monet

   S T A I N P R E _____

2. William Faulkner, Edna Ferber, Jack London

   H A T U R S O _____

3. Sally Ride, Neil Armstrong, Alan Shepard

   S T N S A O R U A T _____

4. Matthew Henson, William Clark, Marco Polo

   R L X R O E P E S _____

5. Dolly Madison, Eleanor Roosevelt, Nancy Reagan

   S R F T I   D A L S E I _____

SALLY RIDE

C. Use a biographical dictionary to find information about one of the people mentioned on this page. On the back of this sheet, write three facts about that person.

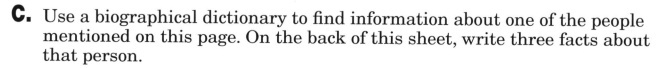

REFERENCE REVIEW: A SCAVENGER HUNT

The library reference shelf has many materials that will help you research a topic, write a report, or just answer a question.

A. Which reference book would you use to answer each question? Choose a source from the box. Then, on the line, write the abbreviation shown in parentheses.

(D)	**dictionary**	**(E)**	**encyclopedia**
(AT)	**atlas**	**(T)**	**thesaurus**
(AL)	**almanac**	**(BD)**	**biographical dictionary**
(RG)	***Readers' Guide to Periodical Literature***		

1. _____ Name three African nations that border the Mediterranean Sea.

2. _____ What high school did Michael Jackson attend?

3. _____ What magazine has a story about rock climbing?

4. _____ How do you pronounce *boisterous*?

5. _____ Who won the 1973 Nobel Prize for chemistry?

6. _____ When was author Beverly Cleary born?

7. _____ How fast can a cheetah run?

8. _____ How many suicides took place in 2006?

9. _____ When was the gas mask invented and how does it work?

10. _____ What is the meaning of *skullduggery*?

11. _____ How long is a *nanosecond*?

12. _____ What three words are synonyms for *lazy*?

13. _____ What state is directly south of Kansas?

14. _____ Who played on the 2007 NBA All-Star team?

15. _____ What brand of color TV does *Consumer Reports* magazine recommend?

B. On the back of this sheet, answer any three questions from *Part A*.

REFERENCE: The Bibliography

You will often be asked to include a *bibliography* with a report or term paper. A bibliography is an *alphabetized* list of the books, reference books, or periodicals that you used to find information. Write down the facts about each source as you use it. You do not want to make a later trip to the library just to find that information. Read the bibliography below. Notice the information listed and the punctuation used.

BOOK→   Abel, Linda. <u>Susan B. Anthony: First Woman to Vote</u>. New York: Dixson Publishing Co., 2002.

ENCYCLOPEDIA→   "Anthony, Susan B.," <u>Concord Encyclopedia</u>, Vol. 1. Boston: Concord Press, 2005, p. 172.

MAGAZINE→   Wright, Carl G. "Great Ladies." *Historical Times,* June 2003, vol. 14, p. 12.

A. Reread the three bibliography entries. Then circle a word or words to correctly complete each sentence.

1. Bibliography entries are in (no special order / alphabetical order).

2. If the entry is more than one line long, the second line is (capitalized / indented).

3. The title of a magazine article is (enclosed in quotation marks / written in capital letters).

4. The title of a book is (enclosed in quotation marks / underlined).

5. An encyclopedia listing begins with the (encyclopedia name / topic).

6. A (comma / colon) is written between the place of publication and the publisher's name.

7. A (period / comma) follows the author's name.

B. Use reference materials in a library or your classroom to make a bibliography with at least four entries. Write your entries in alphabetical order on the back of this sheet.

FOLLOWING WRITTEN DIRECTIONS

From taking a test to baking a cake, careful attention to directions can make a big difference in the outcome! Before beginning a task, always read directions completely—from beginning to end.

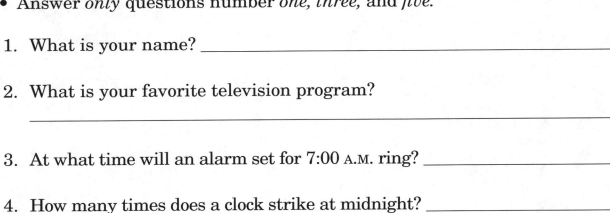

A. Read and follow the directions for this quiz.

QUIZ DIRECTIONS:
- Write your answers *under* the lines.
- Answer *only* questions number *one, three,* and *five.*

1. What is your name? _____

2. What is your favorite television program?

   _____

3. At what time will an alarm set for 7:00 A.M. ring? _____

4. How many times does a clock strike at midnight? _____

5. What event do Americans celebrate on July 4?

   _____

6. Who wrote *The Autobiography of Benjamin Franklin?*

   _____

B. Study *all* the following directions. Read everything to the bottom of the sheet *before* you begin this activity. Write answers upside down on the back of this sheet.

1. In what city is the Brooklyn Bridge?

2. How many fingers are on your left hand?

3. How many questions are on this test?

4. Which president does the Lincoln Memorial honor?

5. What is the sum of 6, 7, 8, and 9?

Do not answer the questions above. Write only your name on the back of this sheet.

FOLLOWING SPOKEN DIRECTIONS

Many times you must follow spoken directions. Before you begin any task, listen carefully to *all* directions. Don't stop listening until the speaker has stopped talking. If you don't understand what you have heard, ask questions.

Simon says, "Put your left hand up."

A. Pair up with a classmate. One partner will read the following directions aloud. The other partner will follow them.

DIRECTIONS TO THE LISTENER:

Follow the oral directions for each item. Do not ask questions or ask the speaker to repeat anything. Turn this sheet over now. Write your responses on the back.

DIRECTIONS TO THE SPEAKER:

Read each of these items aloud once. Give your partner time to do as directed. Do not answer questions.

1. Write your name, first name first, in the upper left-hand corner. Leave off the last letter of your last name.

2. Write today's date in numbers, using dashes between the numbers.

3. Write the number of an hour when both hands of the clock are in the same spot.

4. Write the numbers 5, 10, 15, 12, and 20, and circle the largest number.

5. If you circled 12, draw a circle. If not, draw a star.

6. What is the sum of 4 + 2? Write an incorrect answer.

B. Review the results of *Part A*. Then answer these questions on the back of this sheet.

1. How many directions did the listener respond to exactly as directed?

2. How many directions did the listener complete incorrectly?

3. What could the speaker have done to improve communication?

4. What could the listener have done to improve his or her results?

5. Would the results have been different if the listener had asked questions? If so, why?

TAKING NOTES FROM READING: MAPPING

Taking notes can help you understand and remember what you read. One way to take notes is to *map* ideas. Mapping lets you "picture" main points and show how they relate to one another. Read the paragraph below and study the mapping example. Notice that the key idea is at the center. Supporting points branch out around the main idea.

> The ancient Chinese were remarkable inventors. By cutting letters, or characters, into animal bones, they created one of the oldest written histories. They wove threads spun by silkworms into the first silk. They invented paper by pounding bark fibers into sheets. The Chinese thinker, Confucius, developed a program of testing for government jobs. It became the world's first civil service system.

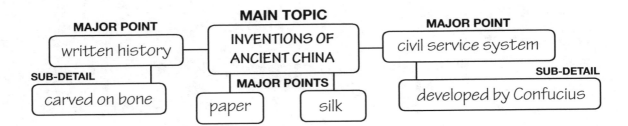

MAIN TOPIC

MAJOR POINT
written history

SUB-DETAIL
carved on bone

INVENTIONS OF ANCIENT CHINA

MAJOR POINTS
paper   silk

MAJOR POINT
civil service system

SUB-DETAIL
developed by Confucius

A. Read the following paragraph. Then, in the space below, map the paragraph. Use the example above as a model.

> More than 2,000 years ago, Emperor Cheng of China built a wall to protect his land. He feared invasion by the Huns, warriors from the north. Cheng forced millions of men to work on the wall. After 10 years, the wall was complete. The Great Wall of China, the longest wall ever built, still stands today.

MAIN TOPIC

B. Select a paragraph or short section of a magazine article or encyclopedia entry. Map the main ideas on the back of this sheet.

TAKING NOTES FROM READING: MORE MAPPING PRACTICE

Remember to follow all three steps when mapping your notes:

(1) Write the *main topic* in the middle of your paper and circle it.

(2) List each *major point* in a smaller circle that branches out from the main idea.

(3) List any *sub-detail* in a circle that connects to a major point.

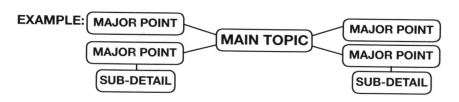

A. Read this paragraph. In the space below, map out your notes.

As humans, we belong to a class of animals called mammals. All mammals share certain traits or characteristics. Most are covered with hair. The mothers' bodies make milk to nourish their young. Most types of mammals live on land. Dolphins and seals, however, are two examples of ocean mammals.

B. Check your understanding of mapping. Study the notes mapped out below. Then, on the back of this sheet, use the information shown in the notes to write a paragraph.

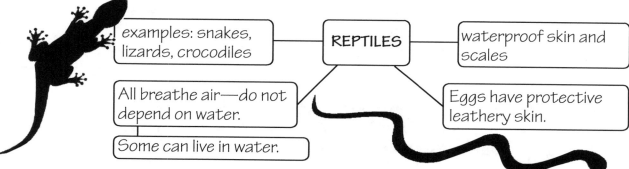

TAKING NOTES FROM READING: Outlining

Outlining is a useful method of taking notes. When you make an outline, you identify the main idea and major points to separate them from less important information. Study the outline form below:

I. **MAIN IDEA**
   A. Major point
   B. Major point
   C. Major point

A. Read the paragraph. Write the main idea after Roman numeral I. Write major points after the capital letters A, B, C, and D.

DREAMLAND: REM SLEEP

Most of our dreams take place during a stage of sleep that scientists call REM. The letters stand for *rapid eye movement.* Quick eye motions under closed lids show that a sleeper is dreaming. Sleepers spend about one-fourth of the night in REM sleep. Near morning, when dreams come more clearly and frequently, REM times get longer. Some scientists believe that the body can't move during REM sleep. That feature may protect sleepers from acting out their dreams.

I. _____

   A. _____

   B. _____

   C. _____

   D. _____

B. Select a paragraph from any classroom textbook. Use outlining to take notes on the information. Make sure you include the paragraph's main idea and major points. Write your outline on the back of this sheet.

TAKING NOTES FROM READING: MORE OUTLINING PRACTICE

In an outline, major points are usually developed with supporting details.
Study the example.

EXAMPLES: **I.** Main Idea
      A. Major point
        1. Detail
        2. Detail

I. Minerals Promote Health
     A. Calcium, an important mineral
       1. Builds bones and teeth
       2. Helps muscles and nerves work

A. Read the paragraph below. Complete the outline
with details under the major points.

> The bumps that cover your tongue are sensitive
> nerve cells called taste buds. They send messages to the brain that
> tell what food tastes like. Taste buds are stimulated by liquid. Food
> must become wet before you can taste it. The buds on different parts of
> your tongue are sensitive to five tastes—sweet, sour, bitter, salty and
> umami. Taste buds on the front and sides of the tongue, for example,
> react to salt. Those on the back of the tongue sense bitter tastes.

I. Taste buds
   A. Nerve cells that cover tongue
      1. _____
      2. _____

   B. Different taste buds sense sweet, sour, bitter, salty, or umami tastes
      1. _____
      2. _____

B. Study the information in the following outline. Write a paragraph
on the back of this sheet.

I. Body senses as warning devices

   A. Discomfort signals danger
     1. Pain of toothache says go to dentist
     2. Heat says avoid fire
   B. Messages from nose and tongue
     1. Smell of gas means get away
     2. Foul taste means food has gone bad

STREAMLINING YOUR NOTES

The purpose of notes is to record important ideas and details for later use.
A few hints can help you streamline your notes and save time.

A. To save time and space, use common *abbreviations* and *symbols*. Write a letter to match each abbreviation or symbol on the left with its meaning on the right.

For assistance call

1-800-ASK-USPS

1. ____ &   a. government
2. ____ w/   b. number
3. ____ i.e.   c. and
4. ____ govt.   d. with
5. ____ w/o   e. without
6. ____ #   f. that is

B. What other abbreviations and symbols do you know? Write a symbol or abbreviation for each of the following words and phrases. If you need to, create a symbol or abbreviation of your own.

1. equals _____   3. department _____

2. and so forth _____   4. for, four _____

C. Always write notes in your own words. Read the following sentences. Record the main ideas in as few words as possible. To shorten words, use abbreviations and symbols. The first one has been done for you. Write notes for sentences 2 and 3 on the back of this sheet.

1. On April 18, 1906, a huge earthquake hit the city of San Francisco, leaving thousands homeless and much of the city in ruins.

   S.F. quake—4/18/06 = 1000s homeless, city wrecked

2. Writer Jack London lived a life of adventure that included stealing oysters on San Francisco Bay, hopping rides on freight trains, and joining the Klondike gold rush of 1897.

3. The first World Series of major league baseball was held in 1903 when the American League's Boston Pilgrims played the National League's Pittsburgh Pirates.

TAKING NOTES WHILE LISTENING

Whether you're reading or listening, you can use the same methods to take notes. *Outlining* works well when you're listening to a lecture. *Mapping* may be better for an informal discussion. To take notes while listening, follow these hints:

(1) Spend most of your time listening. Don't get so busy taking notes that you forget to listen.

(2) Listen for main ideas and write them down. The speaker may indicate a main idea by raising his or her voice, slowing down, or pausing.

(3) Write words and phrases rather than complete sentences. Use symbols and abbreviations. Write notes that make sense to you.

A. Reread the information above. Then write **T** or **F** to show whether each statement below is **true** or **false**.

1. _____ Good notes are always written in complete sentences.

2. _____ Sometimes a speaker pauses to indicate a main idea.

3. _____ You should try to write down a speaker's exact words.

4. _____ Outlining is one useful way to take notes while listening.

B. Pair up with a classmate. One partner will read the following paragraph aloud. The other partner will take notes on the information.

DIRECTIONS TO THE LISTENER: Outline or map notes on the back of this sheet as your partner reads the paragraph aloud.

DIRECTIONS TO THE SPEAKER: First read the following paragraph to yourself. Then read it aloud to your partner.

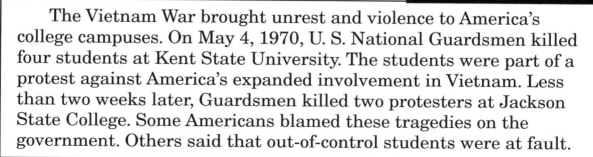

The Vietnam War brought unrest and violence to America's college campuses. On May 4, 1970, U. S. National Guardsmen killed four students at Kent State University. The students were part of a protest against America's expanded involvement in Vietnam. Less than two weeks later, Guardsmen killed two protesters at Jackson State College. Some Americans blamed these tragedies on the government. Others said that out-of-control students were at fault.

C. With your partner, review the notes that were written for *Part B*. Then answer these questions on the back of this sheet: (1) What note taking method did the listener use? (2) What main ideas, if any, were missing from the notes? (3) How could the listener have improved the notes?

ACTIVE LISTENING

Hearing comes naturally, but *listening* doesn't. You can greatly improve your listening skills by remembering a few do's and do not's.

DO'S	DO NOT'S
● **Do** concentrate! Avoid daydreaming. ● **Do** ask questions! Be an involved, active listener. ● **Do** try to picture what the speaker is saying. ● **Do** tune in at the very beginning. Look for the main idea in the opening words.	● **Do not** try to listen and do something else. Listening is a full-time job. ● **Do not** think of what you might say next while others are speaking. ● **Do not** give in to distractions. Recognize them. Learn to listen in spite of them.

A. Stay silent for one minute and **listen**. On the line below, list the sounds you heard that distracted you from listening *(for example: outside traffic noise)*.

_____

B. Pair up with a classmate. One partner will be the speaker. The other will be the listener.

   DIRECTIONS TO THE LISTENER: Review the advice in the chart above. Then turn this sheet over. **Do not** read the class assignment below. As your partner reads, listen carefully without taking notes.

   DIRECTIONS TO THE SPEAKER: Take the role of teacher. Read this class assignment aloud:

> "Now, class, for tonight's homework, read Chapter 3 in your science text. You will learn how running water can generate electricity. Go over the 10 key words listed before the chapter. There will be a vocabulary quiz tomorrow. We will also do an experiment tomorrow, so please bring a key, a rubber band, and a toothpick to class. Do you understand?"

C. If you were the **speaker**, answer these questions on the back of this sheet:

   1. Did you feel you had your listener's attention? What made you think you did or did not?
   2. Describe any distractions you noticed as you spoke.
   3. Did your listener ask questions? If so, what were they?

If you were the **listener**, answer these questions on the back of this sheet:

   1. What chapter will you read tonight?
   2. What two activities should you expect tomorrow?
   3. Would note taking have helped you? How might it have helped?

MORE HINTS FOR ACTIVE LISTENING

No matter how fast someone speaks, our minds move faster. Americans speak at an average rate of about 125 words per minute. Yet people think at about 400 words per minute. No wonder a listener's mind tends to wander! Developing active listening habits will help you keep focused.

A. Put a **plus (+)** by the habits that encourage active listening. Put a **minus (–)** by habits that could get in the way of focused listening.

1. _____   sitting up front, near the speaker

2. _____   sitting next to one's best friend

3. _____   sitting up straight

4. _____   doodling and drawing pictures

5. _____   looking at the speaker

B. A speaker's *body language* can help you decide what to write in your notes. Put a **check (✓)** by *nonverbal clues* that signal a key point.

1. _____   The speaker looks out the window.

2. _____   The speaker makes eye contact with listeners.

3. _____   The speaker writes something on the blackboard.

4. _____   The speaker has been sitting, but now stands up.

5. _____   The speaker has been standing, but now sits down.

C. Certain phrases—like *first of all, most importantly, in summary,* and *the following reasons*—are verbal clues that signal important points. Read the following speech. Underline words and phrases that signal a main point.

Players, we're here to discuss the following problems that face our baseball team. First of all, team members are skipping practice sessions. We've had no pitcher at the last two practices. Our shortstop Brandon nearly threw his arm out trying to get a pitch over the plate. Secondly, there's a lack of teamwork. We need to pull together. Most importantly—we need pride. Clean up those uniforms, tuck in those shirts, and look like real ball players!

NOTE TAKING: Paraphrasing Information

Putting an author's writing into your own words is called *paraphrasing*. Paraphrasing helps you understand the material. It helps you condense the information—keeping the main points and weeding out less important ones.

A. Paraphrase and condense each of the following amendments to the U.S. Constitution. Make sure you keep the main idea as you rewrite the amendment in your own words. The first one has been done for you.

1. In all criminal prosecutions, the accused shall enjoy the right to a speedy and public trial.

   Anyone charged with a crime has the right to a trial.

2. Neither slavery nor involuntary servitude shall exist within the United States.

   _____

3. The right of citizens to vote shall not be denied by the United States or by any state on account of sex.

   _____

B. Practice condensing information. On the back of this sheet, write telegrams reporting each emergency described below. Use as few words as possible. The first one has been done for you.

1. Winds of hurricane force are approaching at rapid velocities and will soon make landfall in this area. It is suggested that all persons seek shelter immediately.

   Hurricane coming. Take cover.

2. Elevated temperatures and blistering breezes have increased the likelihood that brush fires will threaten buildings on the northern fringes of the urban area. Residents are urged to moisten the exteriors of their dwellings.

3. The elevated structure that spans the Wilson River has weakened to the extent that it will no longer support the weight of vehicles. Motorists in that vicinity are advised to seek an alternate route of travel.

NOTE TAKING: RECOGNIZING RELEVANT AND IRRELEVANT INFORMATION

Relevant details are those that support the main idea. When you take notes, record only relevant information. Weed out any information that is *irrelevant* (does *not* support the main idea).

A. Circle the letter of the item that is irrelevant to each main idea listed below. The first one has been done for you.

1. Household pets:
   (a.) tigers   b. goldfish   c. dogs   d. hamsters

2. Things that cause pollution:
   a. factories   b. cars   c. chemicals   d. sun

3. Fattening things:
   a. candy   b. french fries   c. rain   d. milkshakes

4. Modern inventions:
   a. computer   b. cellular phone   c. stagecoach   d. airbags

B. Read the following sentences. Circle the number of the sentence that is irrelevant to the main idea.

   MAIN IDEA: Steps that can prevent accidents at home

1. Automobile drivers and passengers should fasten their seatbelts.

2. Keep a fire extinguisher handy to put out kitchen fires.

3. Carefully clean kitchen tools and counters to avoid spreading germs.

4. Lock medicine cabinets to keep pills away from children.

5. Electricity and water don't mix, so keep hairdryers away from bathtubs and sinks.

C. Read the following paragraph. Find the sentence that is irrelevant to its main idea. Circle the number of that sentence.

(1) A few safety tips can make biking more fun. **(2)** Since any ride can end in a bad fall, a rider should wear a helmet at all times. **(3)** Bicyclists share the road with cars and should obey all traffic rules. **(4)** Bicycle brakes must always be in perfect working order. **(5)** The new 26-inch Road Racer is one of the fastest bikes around. **(6)** For maximum safety, a bicyclist should ride only during daylight hours.

NAME _____   DATE _____

NOTE TAKING REVIEW

Do you remember the five note taking methods: symbols, mapping, outlining, and paraphrasing?

A. Unscramble the letters to form a word that match each example.

EXAMPLE: **WORD:**

1.

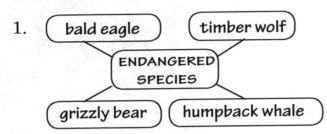

P I M A G N P

_ _ _ _ _ _⬚_

2. I. Endangered species
      A. Bald eagle
         1. Killed by ranchers
         2. Its environment
             polluted by pesticides
      B. Humpback whale
         1. Killed by whale hunters
         2. Meat sold to feed
             humans and pets

T L N I G O N U I

⬚_ _ _ _ _ _ _ _

3. dept., biol., U.S.A.

T A B A B O I S N V I E R

_ _ _ _ _ _ _ _ _⬚_ _ _ _

4. Individuals who reside in transparent abodes should restrain from hurling boulders.

People who live in glass houses shouldn't throw stones.

R A S P P A H R E A

_ _ _ _ _ _ _ _⬚_

5. +   =   w/o   &

B L O S M Y S   _ _ _ _ _ _⬚_

B. Notice the circled letters in *Part A*. To answer the riddle, write the letters in order on the lines.

What can help a student understand information, recognize main points, prepare for tests, and collect information for reports?

ANSWER: ___ ___ ___ ___ ___

Study Skills 1 • © Saddleback Educational Publishing • www.sdlback.com

USING CONTEXT TO CLUE MEANING

You can often tell what an unfamiliar word means by how it is used. The *context*, or surrounding words, can give clues to a new word's meaning.

A. The boldfaced word in each sentence is not a real word. However, its context gives clues to its meaning. Read each sentence. Then circle the best meaning for the boldfaced nonsense word.

1. After dinner the chef brought out a creamy, fattening **lamadora**.

   a. cigar   b. dessert   c. napkin

2. The music played on, and we **twaddled** until our feet were sore.

   a. sang   b. argued   c. danced

3. The forecast called for **blorps**, but I never needed my umbrella.

   a. heat waves   b. showers   c. fog

4. I've always feared **snorblets**, those crawling, hissing creatures.

   a. snakes   b. dogs   c. burglars

B. Use context clues to determine the meanings of real words. Circle the best meaning of the boldfaced word.

1. I **abhor** bullies who pick on people weaker than they are.

   a. befriend   b. admire   c. hate

2. That naughty child often **pilfers** coins from his mother's purse.

   a. polishes   b. counts   c. steals

3. Her blank stare and silly comments make her seem **vacuous**.

   a. adventurous   b. stupid   c. attractive

4. The **orator** turned to the audience, glanced at his notes, cleared his throat, and began to speak.

   a. speaker   b. magician   c. musician

C. Invent a meaning for each nonsense word below. On the back of this sheet, write a sentence using each word. Make sure that the *context* gives clues to the word's meaning.

1. clottered   2. walpert   3. restumpulate

CONTEXT CLUES: Definition

Sometimes the *context* will give you the *definition* of a word. For example, do you know what an "echinoderm" is? You can find its definition in the following sentence: A starfish is an *echinoderm,* an animal with spiny skin.

A. Underline the words in each item below that are clues to the meaning of the boldfaced word. The first one has been done for you.

1. **Mollusks**, or <u>soft-bodied animals</u>, include clams, squid, and slugs.

2. Jill is **bilingual**, able to speak two languages.

3. The neighbors painted their house **ocher**, a dark yellow color.

4. The chef prepared a salad of **alligator pear**, also known as avocado.

5. Sam was **bankrupt**. In other words, he was unable to pay his debts.

B. Read the paragraph for context clues. Then write the meaning of each boldfaced word.

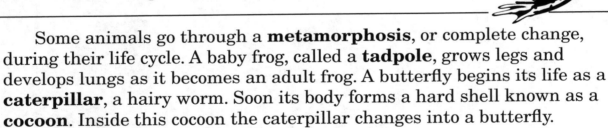

Some animals go through a **metamorphosis**, or complete change, during their life cycle. A baby frog, called a **tadpole**, grows legs and develops lungs as it becomes an adult frog. A butterfly begins its life as a **caterpillar**, a hairy worm. Soon its body forms a hard shell known as a **cocoon**. Inside this cocoon the caterpillar changes into a butterfly.

1. **metamorphosis** = _____

2. **tadpole** = _____

3. **caterpillar** = _____

4. **cocoon** = _____

C. On the back of this sheet, write one sentence for each of the following words. Provide the **definition** of the word within the context of each sentence. (If you don't know what the word means, check a dictionary.)

1. adolescent   2. flexible   3. joggled

CONTEXT CLUES: Examples

A word's context may provide an *example* as a clue to meaning.
In this sentence an example suggests the meaning of *timidity*:

> *He showed his **timidity** by hiding under the bed during a lightning storm.*

From the context, you know that *timidity* has something to do with being fearful.

A. An example suggests the meaning of each boldfaced word below. Circle the letter of the best meaning.

1. Sleeping until noon is just one example of his **sloth**.

   a. laziness   b. intelligence   c. bravery

2. That store sells all kinds of **confections**, such as lollipops, gumballs, licorice drops, and chocolates.

   a. toys   b. sweets   c. sporting goods

3. His boss said that one more **blunder**, like breaking a dish or spilling water, would mean the end of his career.

   a. mistake   b. theft   c. argument

4. A hearty laugh and wide grin are signs of a **jocund** nature.

   a. cruel   b. selfish   c. jolly

5. He had several **monikers**, such as Jack, John, and Jackson.

   a. addresses   b. hobbies   c. names or nicknames

B. Use context clues to help you write a definition for each italicized word.

1. He was especially proud of two *ancestors*, his grandfather and his great-aunt.

   _____

2. Bald spots on its head and back were signs that the bird was *molting*.

   _____

C. On the back of this sheet, write one sentence for each of the following words. Use examples as clues to word meanings. (If you don't know what the word means, check a dictionary.)

1. sludge   2. embezzler   3. solitary

CONTEXT CLUES: Comparison or Contrast

A writer may give clues to a word's meaning by *comparing* or *contrasting* it with something else. A mental picture of something *similar* or *different* can help you guess what a word means.

EXAMPLES:

Her jacket was *downy,* like the fluff of baby chicks.
(This *comparison* suggests that *downy* means extremely soft.)

A rose smells sweet, but a marigold is quite *malodorous.*
(This *contrast* suggests that *malodorous* means bad-smelling.)

A. Read each sentence. Write **comparison** or **contrast** to tell which type of context clue is given. The first one has been done for you.

1. _comparison_   His muscles are as **flaccid** as a jellyfish.

2. _____   Although parking here is **prohibited** on Mondays, it is allowed all other days.

3. _____   Her **crimson** fingernails looked like ten shining rubies.

4. _____   I thought the movie was **enthralling**, but my friends thought it was boring.

5. _____   While cotton wrinkles badly, **dacron** is wrinkle-free.

6. _____   The **cadence** of the breaking waves was as regular as a drumbeat.

7. _____   The **catwalk** over the ship's engine room was similar to a narrow bridge.

B. The words and phrases listed below often signal a comparison or contrast. Reread the sentences in *Part A*. Circle any of these "signal" words or phrases as you find them.

COMPARISON: *as, similar to, like, in the same way*

CONTRAST: *although, on the contrary, but, while, on the other hand*

C. Use context clues to define each boldfaced word in *Part A*. Write your definitions on the back of this sheet.

USING CONTEXT TO CLUE MEANING: A REVIEW

Remember, *context* clues are the familiar words, sentences, and phrases that surround an unfamiliar word. As you read, learn to use context clues to figure out word meanings.

A. Which kind of context clue suggests the meaning of each boldfaced word below? Write **definition**, **example**, **comparison**, or **contrast** on the line.

1. _____ The zoo had an exhibit of **nocturnal** creatures, like bats and owls.

2. _____ You might think a snake's skin is **slimy**, but it is quite pleasantly dry.

3. _____ The ring was made of **garnets**, deep-red stones.

4. _____ His eyes are as **azure** as the sky on a sunny day.

5. _____ Unlike her outgoing friends, Meg is an **introvert**.

B. Write a letter to match each word on the left with its meaning on the right. Use the context clues in *Part A* for help.

1. ____ **garnets**   a. awake and active at night

2. ____ **azure**   b. disagreeably wet and slippery

3. ____ **slimy**   c. clear, deep-red stones used in jewelry

4. ____ **nocturnal**   d. a clear, bright blue color

5. ____ **introvert**   e. one who likes to be alone with his or her own thoughts and feelings

C. On the back of this sheet, write a sentence for each of the following words. In each sentence, suggest the word's meaning with the *kind* of context clue listed. (If you don't know what the word means, check a dictionary.)

1. **brunch** (Use a *definition* to suggest meaning.)

2. **insomnia** (Use an *example* to suggest meaning.)

3. **arid** (Use a *comparison* to suggest meaning.)

4. **survivor** (Use a *contrast* to suggest meaning.)

A MATTER OF CONTEXT

A word's meaning may change with its context. For example, think about the word *yarn* as applied to knitting. Then think about *yarn* as applied to storytelling. Notice how the word's meaning totally changes depending on the context:

I planned to knit the sweater out of yellow *yarn.*

The old man told a *yarn* about his adventures panning for gold.

A. Each boldfaced word below refers to a certain subject. Using context to clue meaning, draw a line to match each sentence on the left with a subject on the right.

1. The **shuttle** crew prepared for the long flight.

    a. weaving

2. The **shuttle** carried the thread back and forth across the loom.

    b. space travel

3. He knocked down the last two pins and scored a **spare**.

    a. automotives

4. Don't worry about the flat tire; we have a **spare**.

    b. bowling

5. The storm left the yard covered with pine **needles**.

    a. trees

6. The fabric store sold all sizes of **needles**.

    b. sewing

B. On the back of this sheet, write two sentences for each boldfaced word. Provide context clues to suggest meanings for the words as they would apply to each subject.

1. **stern** (personalities, ships)

2. **capsule** (medicine, space travel)

3. **strike** (baseball, labor unions)

4. **mouse** (animals, computers)

     Study Skills 1 • © Saddleback Educational Publishing • www.sdlback.com

UNLOCKING WORD MEANING: PREFIXES, SUFFIXES, AND ROOTS

Many words in our language are made up of a combination of three parts—*prefixes, suffixes,* and *roots.* Prefixes come at the front of words. Suffixes come at the end of words. Roots are the main parts of words to which prefixes and suffixes are attached.

EXAMPLE: p r e s c h o o l e r a child who does not yet go to school

PREFIX	ROOT	SUFFIX
meaning before		meaning a person or thing that does something

A. Underline the *root* of each word. The first one has been done for you.

1. <u>color</u>less
2. homeless
3. prepay
4. joyful
5. counting
6. discounted
7. recalled
8. preview
9. freezer
10. stranger
11. healthful
12. unhealthy

B. A word *root* usually keeps the same meaning, even when used in different words. Study the common roots and their meanings listed in the box below. Then circle the letter of the item that correctly completes each definition.

port: carrying	*geo:* earth	*tele:* distance	*verb:* word	*astro:* star

1. transportation: a system of
   a. carrying things from one place to another
   b. changing things from one shape into another
   c. making things disappear

2. astrology: the study of
   a. the earth   b. the stars   c. living creatures

3. verbalize: to express an idea in
   a. a drawing   b. spoken word   c. music

C. Each word below contains a root listed in *Part B.* Try to guess what each word means. Then look it up in a dictionary. Write a definition for each word on the back of the sheet.

verbatim   geologic   telepathy   astronaut   reporter

UNLOCKING WORD MEANING: Prefixes

You can completely change a word's meaning by adding a *prefix* at the beginning. The prefix *un-* means *not.* Watch what happens when you add *un-* to the beginning of a word:

un + important = unimportant (not important)

A. Underline the prefix in each boldfaced word below. Then circle the letter of the prefix meaning. The first one has been done for you.

1. **replay**   a. before   ⓑ again   c. not
2. **bicycle**   a. one   b. two   c. under
3. **nonsense**   a. not   b. in front of   c. three
4. **superhuman**   a. more than   b. after   c. less than

B. Study each word below. If it has a prefix, write the **prefix**, a **plus sign (+)**, and the **root** on the line. If the word is *not* made of a root and prefix, write an **X**. (*Hint:* A root must make sense without the prefix.) The first one has been done for you.

1. unmarked _un + marked_   5. ink _____

2. united _____   6. invisible _____

3. preflight _____   7. misbehave _____

4. precious _____   8. mister _____

C. Add a prefix from the box to create a word that matches each meaning. The first one has been done for you.

| bi   post   pre   re   tri |

1. **ROOT WORD: game**   p r e g a m e (before the game)
   p o s t g a m e (after the game)

2. **ROOT WORD: cycle**   __ __ __ __ __ __ __ (two-wheeled cycle)
   __ __ __ __ __ __ __ (three-wheeled cycle)

3. **ROOT WORD: view**   __ __ __ __ __ __ __ (look at ahead of time)
   __ __ __ __ __ __ (look at again)

D. On the back of this sheet, write a word that begins with each of the following prefixes: *pre, post, re, super, un.*

UNLOCKING WORD MEANING: SUFFIXES

You can change the meaning of a root word by adding a *suffix* at the end. The suffix -*less* means *without*. Notice how adding -*less* to a root word changes its meaning:

hope + *less* = hopeless (without hope)

Adding a suffix may change a word's part of speech. Notice how *hope,* a noun, became *hopeless,* an adjective.

A. Use a suffix from the box to make a *noun* of each *verb* in parentheses. Write the noun on the line. Use a dictionary if you need help spelling the new word.

ation	ers	ion	ists

1. Have you heard of a coral (form) _____ called the Great Barrier Reef?

2. The South Pacific is a perfect (locate) _____ for coral to grow.

3. Each year the Great Barrier Reef attracts many (tour) _____ to Australia.

4. (Swim) _____ can enjoy the warm, calm waters around the reef.

5. Scientists worry that water (pollute) _____ might damage the delicate reef.

B. The suffixes -*er* and -*est* are used to compare things. Replace each phrase in parentheses with a single word. Write the word on the line.

1. The flea is one of the (most clever) _____ creatures.

2. Fleas can jump (more high) _____ than most insects.

3. Fleas are (more smart) _____ than you would imagine.

4. A circus of trained fleas may be one of the world's (most strange) _____ sights.

C. Create nouns by adding -*ness* to each of these adjectives: *weird, great, kind.* Then write a sentence for each new noun. Do your work on the back of this sheet.

WORD PARTS: CHECK YOUR UNDERSTANDING

Use what you know about *roots, prefixes,* and *suffixes* to unlock meaning.

A. Separate each boldfaced word into its parts. Write any **prefix(es)**, plus the **root word**, plus any **suffix(es)**. Then circle the letter of the word or phrase that best defines the word. The first one has been done for you.

1. The saxophone music was sweet and **soulful**.

   _____soul_____ + _____ful_____

   (a.) full of deep feeling   b. empty of meaning

2. The doctor said she needed some **relaxation**.

   _____ + _____

   a. peaceful rest   b. challenging work

3. I was **semiawake** and only heard part of the lecture.

   _____ + _____

   a. sound asleep   b. half asleep

4. The school newspaper comes out **bimonthly**.

   _____ + _____ + _____

   a. once a month   b. twice a month

5. The coffee roasters planned to **decaffeinate** all their beans.

   _____ + _____ + _____

   a. to remove caffeine   b. to sell quickly

6. The ghost that had disappeared **rematerialized** before my eyes.

   _____ + _____ + _____

   a. suddenly disappeared   b. took shape again

B. Read the following paragraph. On the back of this sheet, divide each **boldfaced** word into its parts. Then write the meaning of each word.

> The **stranger** entered the room. I became **uncomfortable** when he looked at me. The blood pounded in my head, and I felt my face **redden**. Could this **visitor** be a **supernatural** being from another world?

BETTER COMPREHENSION: Key Words and Ideas

Identifying *key words and ideas* helps you understand what you read. Once you have picked out a main point, you can relate all other information to it.

**BIG JIM'S
SURPLUS STORE
SALE
April 12–27**

A. Key words give a sentence its meaning. You could remove all the other words in the sentence and still have the main point. List the key words on the line below each sentence. The first one has been done for you.

1. Big Jim's Surplus Store will drastically slash prices during its annual spring clearance sale, which runs from April 12 to April 27.

   Big Jim's Surplus Store sale April 12–27
   _____

2. Luckily, police spotted the robbers' red sports car speeding south on Highway 101 and stopped the fleeing criminals before they could escape.

   _____

3. To please a boss, it is wise to be on time and even better to be early.

   _____

4. Soccer team tryouts will be held this Wednesday at 7:00 in the evening at the Dawson Park soccer field.

   _____

5. Be sure to bring sturdy, waterproof rain gear on the camping trip next weekend, because the National Weather Service forecast calls for occasionally heavy showers and gusty winds.

   _____

B. Once you have learned to identify *key words* in sentences, you will find it easier to pick out the *main idea* in a paragraph. On the back of this sheet, write in your own words the main idea of the following paragraph.

> Many people think raccoons are cute creatures, but they can be destructive pests. These greedy eaters often ruin farm crops with their nightly visits. They rob birds' nests and raid chicken coops. Because raccoons have from six to eight babies at a time, the furry animals can quickly overrun a large area.

IMPROVING UNDERSTANDING: Recognizing Sequence

Information is easier to remember if it is arranged in some kind of *sequence,* or logical order. Making lists is one of the best ways to sequence material in your mind.

A. Write a heading for the information in each of the following sentences. Then list the items in a logical order according to the order in which they happened. The first one has been done for you.

1. Creative inventors gave us televisions, cars, telephones, and computers.

   <u>   Inventions   </u> : <u> telephones, cars, televisions, computers </u>

2. This evening's chores include washing the dinner dishes, preparing dinner, and shopping for groceries.

   _____ : _____

   _____

3. Preparations for the party included decorating the room, blowing up balloons, and buying supplies.

   _____ : _____

   _____

B. Unscramble the events in the following paragraph. Write a number before each sentence to show the order in which the events occurred.

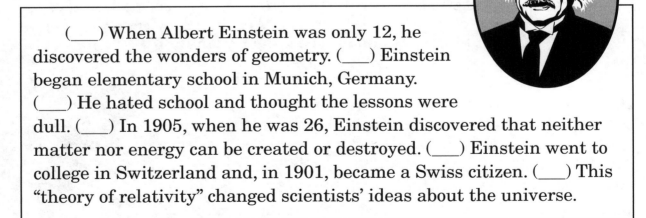

   (___) When Albert Einstein was only 12, he discovered the wonders of geometry. (___) Einstein began elementary school in Munich, Germany. (___) He hated school and thought the lessons were dull. (___) In 1905, when he was 26, Einstein discovered that neither matter nor energy can be created or destroyed. (___) Einstein went to college in Switzerland and, in 1901, became a Swiss citizen. (___) This "theory of relativity" changed scientists' ideas about the universe.

C. Think of a task you know how to do. How many steps does it take to complete it? List the steps in a logical order on the back of this sheet. (*Suggestions:* changing a tire, planning a night on the town, making a sandwich)

PREPARING FOR TESTS

How do you get ready for a test? The strategies you use to prepare can make a big difference in the outcome.

A. Compare the hints below with your own pretest study habits. Put a **check (✓)** beside the methods you already use.

1. _____ Anticipate what material the test will cover and what questions will be asked. Listen in class for clues about what is important.

2. _____ Ask the teacher what *type of questions* (for example, true-false, multiple choice, or essay) will be on the test.

3. _____ Do more than just reread notes or text chapters. Identify key points with an outline or diagram. Highlight ideas that might be covered. Write key words in the margins.

4. _____ Avoid cramming. Begin reviewing *three to six days* before the test. Then you should need only a brief review the night before the test.

5. _____ Make a sample test. Answer the questions yourself or have a friend quiz you.

B. Write **T** or **F** to tell whether each statement is **true** or **false**.

1. _____ You should start studying several days before a test.

2. _____ Try to reread all class assignments the night before the test.

3. _____ It can be helpful to have a friend quiz you.

4. _____ Don't try to guess what the test will cover; study everything!

5. _____ The most important studying occurs the night before a test.

6. _____ It is helpful to know what kind of test you will have.

7. _____ Teachers often give clues about what they will ask on the test.

8. _____ Highlighting ideas and writing margin notes is a waste of time.

C. Review the items you checked off in *Part A*. Think about those you did *not* check. On the back of this sheet, describe two ways you could improve your pretest study methods.

THE TERMINOLOGY OF TESTS

Sharpen your test-taking skills as you review the terms listed in the box.

| ANTICIPATE | CRAM | DIRECTIONS | ESSAY | HIGHLIGHT | OBJECTIVE | MARGIN |

A. To complete the puzzle, match each clue with a term from the word list above.

ACROSS

3. To study many facts in a hurry

   It seldom helps to ____ for a test.

6. To be aware of ahead of time

   Try to ____ questions that will be on the test.

7. A short piece of writing giving the author's ideas

   An ____ test asks students to write about what they know.

DOWN

1. Instructions on how to do something

   Read all ____ before you begin a test.

2. Based on facts about specific information

   ____ test questions have one correct answer.

4. Blank space around the writing on a notebook page

   Write main points in the ____ of your notes.

5. To indicate an important point by shading, coloring, underlining, etc.

   If you ____ key ideas, you are likely to remember them.

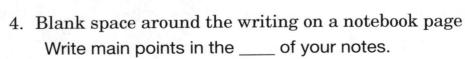

B. Imagine that your teacher has just announced an upcoming test in this class. On the back of this sheet, write three questions you would anticipate finding on the test. Then write the answers to the questions.

TEST-TAKING TIPS

Here are a few strategies to help you do your best work on test day.

A. Read these **ABCs** of test-taking.
Check (✓) habits you already practice.

____ **A**rrive early.

____ **B**ring all materials with you
(pen, paper, eraser, calculator, etc.).

____ **C**arefully listen to the teacher's
directions and comments.

____ **D**on't begin without reading *all* directions.

____ **E**very minute counts, so budget your time.

____ **F**irst answer the questions you are sure about.

____ **G**uess at answers you don't know, unless there is a penalty
for wrong answers.

____ **H**andle objective questions *before* essay questions.

____ **I**f you don't know the answer, put a mark next to the
question. Go back to it later.

____ **J**ust change an answer if you are *sure* it is wrong.

____ **K**now how much time you have and use *all* the time allowed.

B. Circle the letter of the best action to take in each test situation.

1. You are quite sure you know what the teacher wants. You should:
   a. Skip the directions to save time.
   b. Read all the directions anyway.

2. You see objective and essay questions. You should begin with:
   a. the objective questions.   b. the essay questions.

3. You aren't sure about an answer. You should:
   a. leave the question blank.   b. make your best guess.

4. You are finished 10 minutes before the end of class. You should:
   a. stretch, rest, and relax.   b. check your paper for errors.

C. On the back of this sheet, describe one new test-taking strategy
you plan to use.

TAKING A TRUE/FALSE TEST

Tests can be divided into two basic types—*objective tests* and *essay tests.* Usually, an objective question has only one correct answer. The most common kinds of objective questions are *true/false, multiple choice, matching,* and *short answer.*

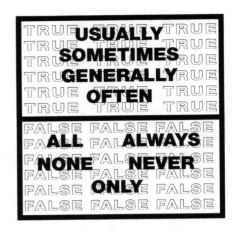

True/false questions ask you to make a judgment. Is the statement correct or incorrect? The best way to do well on a test is to learn the material. However, following a few hints can help you answer true/false questions correctly.

A. Look for the words *all, always, only, none,* or *never.* These words are often used in **FALSE** statements because they are absolute.

On the other hand, key words such as *usually, sometimes, generally,* and *often* allow for exceptions. These words will most often be used in **TRUE** statements.

Read the following statements. Write **T** or **F** to show whether each is **true** or **false**.

1. _____   When studying, it often helps to make an outline from your notes.

2. _____   Always leave test questions blank unless you are sure that you know the correct answer.

3. _____   Studying alone is always better than studying with a group.

4. _____   It is generally a bad idea to cram right before a test.

5. _____   Your first guess is usually your best one.

6. _____   A good student always studies all the material and never asks what type of questions the teacher will ask.

B. Notice the length of each true/false statement. In order for a statement to be true, *all parts of it must be true.* The longer the statement, the more likely it is that part of it is false.

Look back at *Part A.* Then answer these questions:

1. What are the numbers of the two longest statements
   in *Part A?* _____, _____

2. Are these statements *true* or *false?* _____

TAKING A TRUE/FALSE TEST: MORE PRACTICE

Here's more practice to improve your true/false test-taking skills:

A. Review the hints for taking true/false tests. Write **T** or **F** to tell whether each statement below is **true** or **false**.

1. _____ The words *always, all, none*, and *never* usually indicate that a statement is false.

2. _____ The words *usually, sometimes, generally*, and *often* will always make a statement true.

3. _____ A very long statement is more likely to be false.

4. _____ A statement should be considered true if any one part of it is true.

B. When faced with a true/false question, you should *guess* if you don't know the answer! After all, you have a 50 percent chance of answering correctly! Just for fun, write **T** or **F** to tell if each statement below is **true** or **false**. You may not know the answer, but use the hints you've learned to make a good guess. The answers appear at the bottom of the page. Don't peek as you take the test!

1. _____ All people of the Middle East practice the religion of Islam.

2. _____ Islam is one of the world's largest religions.

3. _____ From the west coast to the east coast, the United States has four time zones.

4. _____ States in the Pacific Time Zone include Oregon, Washington, California, Hawaii, and Illinois.

5. _____ Most tornadoes occur in places that have frequent thunderstorms.

6. _____ Tornadoes occur only in the midwestern United States.

7. _____ If you go to a basement, you will be safe during a tornado.

C. Check your answers to *Part B* against the answers at the bottom of the page. Then answer the following questions.

How many questions did you get right? _____

How many of your answers were guesses? _____

ANSWERS TO PART B: (1) F (2) T (3) T (4) F (5) T (6) F (7) F

TAKING A MULTIPLE CHOICE TEST

When asking *objective questions*, teachers are looking for specific answers. Objective tests often include *multiple choice* questions. These questions ask you to choose an answer from a group of possibilities.

TIPS FOR TAKING A MULTIPLE CHOICE TEST

1. Read the questions carefully. Watch for tricky wording such as "Which is *not* an example of..." or "Which is the *incorrect* answer...."

2. Read *all* choices. Sometimes all the choices will be correct, with the final one reading "all of the above."

3. If you aren't sure of the right answer, cross out answers that are clearly wrong. Then pick the best answer from the remaining choices.

4. When you don't know the answer, *guess*. Unless there is a penalty for a wrong guess, you have nothing to lose. The longest answer is often the correct one since it has been written to be complete.

A. Circle the letter of the best answer.

1. When answering a multiple choice question, it is wise to

   a. stop reading the choices once you see the right answer.
   b. answer only if you are sure you are correct.
   c. read all the answers before making your choice.

2. If you aren't sure of the right answer, it is a good idea to

   a. eliminate the clearly wrong choices.
   b. make a good guess.
   c. do both of the above.

3. When answering multiple choice questions, it is *not* a good idea to

   a. take your best guess.
   b. select one answer without reading all the others.
   c. waste time reading the questions carefully.

B. Pick a hobby or topic that you know a lot about. On the back of this sheet, write three multiple choice questions. Your questions should test a person's knowledge of that topic. Include three possible answers for each question.

Study Skills 1 • © Saddleback Educational Publishing • www.sdlback.com

TAKING A MULTIPLE CHOICE TEST: More Practice

It can help to eliminate multiple choice answers that are clearly incorrect. Be on the lookout for an answer that is totally foolish. Narrow down your choices by getting rid of silly statements first!

A. Identify and *cross out* the one answer that is most obviously incorrect. Circle a letter to show the best choice from the remaining answers. The first one has been done for you.

1. Who was Abraham Lincoln?

    a. ~~quarterback for the Detroit Lions~~

    b. the first U.S. president

    (c.) the 16th U.S. president

2. What event does the 4th of July celebrate?

    a. American independence

    b. the arrival of summer

    c. the start of ski season

3. Which animal has a poisonous sting?

    a. dog   b. scorpion   c. rattlesnake

4. What do owls do at night?

    a. hunt   b. sleep

    c. attend rock concerts

5. What should you do when you don't know the answer to an objective test question?

    a. cry   b. guess   c. leave it blank

B. As you read each question, watch for tricky wording. Then circle the letter of the best answer.

1. Which is *not* a good tip for taking multiple choice tests?

    a. Read all the answers before selecting one.

    b. The longest answer is often the correct one.

    c. Don't guess at any answers.

2. Which is an *incorrect* way to treat a cut hand?

    a. Put pressure on the wound.

    b. Shake the hand vigorously.

    c. Clean the wound.

3. In case of an earthquake you should *not*

    a. call 911.

    b. scream for help.

    c. both of the above

    d. neither of the above

4. Which pretest study method is the *least* helpful?

    a. studying all night before a test

    b. beginning to study several nights before the test

    c. making an outline from your notes

TAKING A COMPLETION TEST

Some objective tests ask you to *complete* a sentence by *filling in a blank.* The instructor is usually looking for a specific key word or phrase. The test item may or may not provide you with answer choices.

When you answer completion questions, look for **context clues**:

- Watch for *a* and *an* before the blank. Remember that the word following *an* must begin with a *vowel*. The word following *a* must begin with a *consonant*.

    EXAMPLE: An <u>eyelid</u> protects the human eye from light.

- Look at the *verb* in the sentence. If it is singular, the subject must be singular. If it is plural, the subject must be plural.

    EXAMPLE: Our <u>eyes</u> **are** the sense organs that allow us to see.

A. Complete each statement with an answer from the box. If you don't know the answer, use context clues to help you make a good guess.

brain	iris	light rays	optic nerve	pupil

1. An _____ is the big, colored circle in your eye.

2. The smaller, black circle is called a _____.

3. _____ bounce off objects and carry their image to your eyes.

4. An _____ sends messages away from your eye.

5. Your _____ receives the optic nerve's messages.

B. Read the paragraph below. Then, on the back of this sheet, write three *completion questions* based on the information.

Five senses—sight, hearing, smell, taste, and touch—provide the brain with information about the outside world. Sensing devices called *nerves* are connected to the brain. At the ends of the nerves are *nerve cells* that are sensitive to different things. For example, some nerve cells are sensitive to how things taste. The nerve cells pass information along the nerves to the brain. The brain might receive a message and respond, "That's too salty!"

TAKING A COMPLETION TEST: MORE PRACTICE

Read each completion question several times.
This repetition may help you think of the answer.

A. Complete each statement with an answer
from the box.

an	blank	context	guess

1. Completion test questions ask you to write
   an answer in the _____ space.

2. _____ clues can help you come up with the answer.

3. The word _____ will always be followed by an answer
   that begins with a vowel.

4. As with other types of objective questions, if you don't know the
   answer you should make a _____.

B. Read the statements below. Fill in the best answer you know.

1. A person who searches new regions and makes discoveries is
   called an _____.

2. There are _____ seasons in the year.

3. The Pony Express carried _____ across the country.

4. In 1903, the Wright Brothers made and piloted an _____.

C. Sometimes an item will ask a question and then provide a space
for the answer. Practice answering these questions by filling in
the blanks below.

1. In what year did Columbus sail the ocean blue? _____

2. A spelling rule says *i* before *e,* except after what letter? _____

3. How many days has September? _____

4. Which month of the year is longer in leap year? _____

D. Imagine you are making up a test about using a calendar. On the
back of this sheet, write three completion questions.

TAKING A MATCHING TEST

On a *matching test*, you must choose an item from one list that in some way matches an item from a second list. You may be asked to connect the two items by drawing lines or by numbering one list.

Remember these hints about successfully completing a matching test:

- *Begin by reading the list on the right.* Since it usually contains the answer choices, you will be aware of all the possibilities for answers.

- *First, complete all matches that you know.* Cross off items used on the second list as soon as they are used. This *process of elimination* narrows your choices.

- Once you have *eliminated* the items you were sure of, you should be able to *make a good guess* on the rest.

A. The column on the left lists state names. The column on the right lists well-known tourist attractions. *Draw a line* to match each state with a tourist attraction located there.

1. New York
2. Arizona
3. Florida
4. California

a. Grand Canyon
b. Golden Gate Bridge
c. Statue of Liberty
d. Everglades

B. Write a letter to match each animal on the left with the name of its young on the right.

1. _____ bird
2. _____ dog
3. _____ cat
4. _____ goat
5. _____ elephant
6. _____ lion
7. _____ deer

a. cub
b. kitten
c. kid
d. calf
e. fledgling
f. fawn
g. puppy

C. How good were your guesses? The answers to *Parts A* and *B* are at the bottom of this page. Check your answers. If you got some answers wrong, tell how the hints failed you. If you got all the answers right, tell how—or *if*—the hints helped you. Write your explanations on the back of this sheet.

ANSWERS TO PART A: (1) c (2) a (3) d (4) b   PART B: (1) e (2) g (3) b (4) c (5) d (6) a (7) f

TAKING OBJECTIVE TESTS: A Review

Review what you have learned about objective tests. You will get more right answers if you understand the different *kinds* of questions.

A. Write **T** or **F** to show whether each statement is **true** or **false**.

1. _____ Four common types of objective questions include true/false, multiple choice, essay, and completion.

2. _____ A completion test challenges you to match items in one column with items in a second column.

3. _____ You should read *all* multiple choice options before making your selection.

B. Circle the letter of the best answer.

1. Which is *not* a good hint for preparing for tests?

   a. Start studying several days before a test.

   b. Never eat breakfast before a test.

   c. Make an outline to identify the main points in your notes.

2. On a completion test, the word *a* before a blank clues you that the answer will

   a. begin with a consonant.

   b. begin with a vowel.

   c. be plural.

C. Complete each statement by filling in the blank.

1. On a true/false test, the words *never* and *always* are often clues that a statement is

   _____.

2. The words *usually* and *sometimes* are often clues that a statement is

   _____.

D. Draw a line to match each *kind* of test on the left with a question *example* on the right.

1. true/false

2. multiple choice

3. completion

a. ___ The device used to hit a baseball is called a paddle.

b. The device used to hit a baseball is called a _____.

c. The device used to hit a baseball is called a
a. bat   b. paddle   c. racket

THE VOCABULARY OF ESSAY TESTS

An essay test allows answers that are more *subjective* than those on an objective test. A subjective answer focuses on your own ideas, opinions, and understanding as well as on facts. To answer an essay question, organize what you know and express it in a composition.

ESSAY QUESTION EXAMPLES:

1. **Compare** two characters in *Huckleberry Finn*.

2. **Describe** the effects of global warming on South America's forests.

Look at the words that begin the samples above. An essay question usually starts with or includes a key word. It tells you what *kind* of answer the teacher expects.

KEY WORD	ANSWER REQUIRES YOU TO
describe	create a verbal picture of the topic, to give details or tell about what or how something is
summarize	give a brief account of main ideas without many details
compare	point out similarities and differences between two or more things
contrast	point out differences only
explain	make clear the cause or reason for something
evaluate	weigh positive and negative evidence about something and give your own opinion based on that evidence
criticize	give your opinion based on reasons—including good and bad points
discuss	give reasons for and against something

A. Circle the key word that best introduces each essay question.

1. (Describe / Discuss) Huckleberry Finn's personality.

2. (Contrast / Discuss) a law that would raise the legal driving age to 18.

3. (Summarize / Compare) the Declaration of Independence.

4. (Explain / Criticize) why heavy snowfall increases avalanche danger.

5. (Evaluate / Compare) the traits of a dog with those of a wolf.

B. On the back of this sheet, write an essay question that could appear on a test in this class. Begin your question with a key word from the chart above.

THE VOCABULARY OF ESSAY TESTS: MORE PRACTICE

Be certain that you understand what is being asked in an essay question. Remember to pay attention to *key words* and respond accordingly. For example, *evaluating* something is different than *describing* it, and *comparing* is different than *summarizing*.

A. Circle the hidden words in the puzzle. They may go up, down, across, backward, or diagonally. Check off each word as you find it.

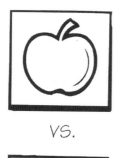

VS.

_____ DESCRIBE

_____ SUMMARIZE

_____ COMPARE

_____ CONTRAST

_____ EXPLAIN

_____ EVALUATE

_____ CRITICIZE

_____ DISCUSS

S	A	N	R	O	J	E	D	L	I
C	U	R	B	R	I	T	I	E	T
C	O	M	P	A	R	E	S	V	R
D	K	N	M	O	N	K	C	A	X
E	L	L	T	A	R	O	U	L	Z
S	Q	U	I	R	R	T	S	U	N
C	A	V	R	O	A	I	S	A	L
R	C	F	H	P	W	S	Z	T	O
I	M	A	N	G	D	O	T	E	T
B	C	R	I	T	I	C	I	Z	E
E	X	P	L	A	I	N	A	M	E

B. Circle a letter to show what each question asks you to do.

1. *Evaluate* your school lunch program.
   a. Tell about both the strong points and the weak points.
   b. Tell about the ingredients of a typical lunch.

2. *Summarize* the school policy on tardiness.
   a. Give your opinion of it.
   b. Give the major points of it.

3. *Contrast* the climate of Nevada with that of Louisiana.
   a. Tell the similarities and differences.
   b. Tell *only* the differences.

4. *Describe* your city's downtown area.
   a. Create a clear picture of it.
   b. Tell how it could be improved.

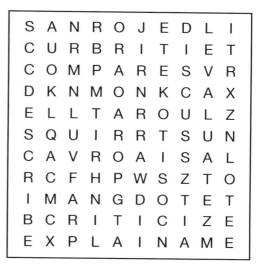

TAKING AN ESSAY TEST

Organizing your essay test answer is just like organizing paragraphs in any composition. You will need to provide main ideas and details to support them. Begin by stating the main idea of your answer. As part of this statement, you can *rephrase* the essay question itself. This will get you started on the right track.

A. Read each essay question below. Then circle the letter of the sentence that would best begin an answer. The first one has been done for you.

1. **Explain** the process of creating electricity from nuclear energy.
   a. Nuclear energy is a clean source of electricity.
   b. Nuclear energy becomes electricity in three major steps.

2. **Contrast** the traits of a bee and a fly.
   a. The bee and the fly are two insects that have very different traits.
   b. Both bees and flies help keep our gardens flowering.

3. **Describe** the character of Juliet in *Romeo and Juliet*.
   a. *Romeo and Juliet* is about two young people who fall deeply in love.
   b. In *Romeo and Juliet*, Shakespeare gives Juliet a complex character.

4. **Evaluate** recent changes in the school sports program.
   a. In my opinion, most of the changes in the school sports program have been improvements.
   b. Our school sports program is much like that of other schools.

B. On the back of this sheet, write a sentence that could begin an answer to each question below. *Hints: Rephrase the question. Make sure you respond to key words.*

1. Summarize the plot of your favorite short story.

2. Evaluate the study area that you usually use.

3. Describe the study area that you usually use.

4. Compare the traits of the common house cat with those of a tiger.

Study Skills 1 • © Saddleback Educational Publishing • www.sdlback.com

TAKING AN ESSAY TEST: FURTHER HINTS

Remember these tips when you answer essay test questions.

A. Put a **check** (✓) beside each test-taking method that you already use. Put an **X** by methods you are still trying to learn.

1. ____ Read all questions before you begin. If you have a choice of questions, select the one you can answer best.

2. ____ Stick to the topic. Only answer *what the questions asks*. Don't try to write everything you know about the subject.

3. ____ Estimate how much time you can spend on each question. Budget your time. Check the time as you work, and stick to your budget!

4. ____ Use complete sentences in your writing.

5. ____ Make an outline to organize your answers. Jot down main ideas and important details before you begin writing.

6. ____ Emphasize your organization with words like *for example, first, secondly, however,* and *in summary.*

7. ____ Restate your major points in a conclusion or summary.

B. Give some thought to this question: *What is the climate like in your region, and how does it affect daily life?* Fill in the blanks on the outline below.

I. Climate of _____ *(a name for your area)*

   A. _____ *(detail)*

   B. _____ *(detail)*

   C. _____ *(detail)*

II. How the climate affects daily life

   A. _____ *(detail)*

   B. _____ *(detail)*

   C. _____ *(detail)*

C. Use the outline in *Part B* to write an essay answer on the back of this sheet. Write two paragraphs, one for each outline heading. Begin the answer by *rephrasing the question*. Make sure each paragraph has a *topic sentence*.

REVIEWING YOUR TEST

You can learn a lot from a test your teacher returns to you. By studying the mistakes you made, you can be better prepared for future exams.

A. Suppose a teacher has returned the sample test below. Look it over carefully.

TRUE/FALSE

1. _F_   None of the ancient Egyptians believed in gods.

✓ 2. _T_   All Egyptians were buried in golden, jewel-covered coffins.

3. _T_   Most ancient Egyptians worked as simple farmers.

MULTIPLE CHOICE

4. *Pharaoh* means: a. Crown Wearer.   b. The Big Louse.   (c.) The Great House.

✓ 5. The *Nile* is an: a. Egyptian river   b. Greek king   (c.) Mediterranean city

COMPLETION

6. A ___mummy___ is a body treated with chemicals and wrapped in cloth.

✓ 7. An ___pyramid___ system carried water to the fields of Egypt.

ESSAY

8. Compare the Egyptian god *Osiris* with the Greek god *Hades*.

+0   _The ancient Egyptians believed in Osiris, the god of death. They_
     expected to cross a river to the next world when they died. There
     they would meet Osiris. Some pictures show Osiris as a man with an
     elephant's trunk. Others show him with a bull's horns.

B. Now analyze errors in the test. Circle the letter of the best answer.

1. You should have guessed the answer to 2 was *false* because
   a. it used the word *all*.   b. gold had not yet been discovered.

2. You should have chosen item *a* as an answer to 5 because
   a. it is the first choice.   b. the answer must start with a *vowel*.

C. Write the answers to the following questions on the back of this sheet.

1. Explain why a student should have known that *pyramid* was an incorrect answer for question 7.

2. Explain why a teacher would give no credit for the essay answer.

THREE STEPS TO SOLVING PROBLEMS

Question, dilemma, riddle, puzzle—these are all synonyms for the word *problem.* A problem is any situation that needs an answer or a solution. A problem can be a situation involving your friends or your job. It can be a question in your math book or in the science lab.

Use three steps to problem-solving as you consider the design of an everyday object—the telephone.

A. **Step 1: Tell yourself exactly what the *problem* is. Be very specific.**

On the lines below, identify one problem in the design of your household telephone. Read the suggested example. Then come up with a problem of your own.

EXAMPLE: *A person with poor hearing might not hear it ring.*

YOUR TELEPHONE PROBLEM: _____

B. **Step 2: Think of a *strategy* you might use to solve the problem.**

A strategy is *not* the solution to the problem. It is a way to *find* the solution (for example: make a list, talk it over with friends, draw a diagram).

EXAMPLE PROBLEM: *A person with poor hearing might not hear the phone ring.*

EXAMPLE STRATEGY: *Make a list of other senses that could alert the person to a call.*

YOUR TELEPHONE PROBLEM: _____

YOUR STRATEGY: _____

C. **Step three: Use your strategy to come up with a solution.**

SOLUTION TO EXAMPLE PROBLEM: *Add a flashing light to visually indicate that a call is coming in.*

SOLUTION TO YOUR TELEPHONE PROBLEM: _____

_____

If your solution works, you are finished. If it does not, try another strategy. Remember, if you want to solve a problem, you must risk being wrong a few times. Always be ready to try another idea.

PROBLEM-SOLVING PRACTICE

Review the three steps to problem solving:

1. Identify the problem.

2. Think up possible strategies for solving the problem, and choose the one that seems best.

3. Use the strategy to reach a solution.

Remember, many problems do not have one "right" way to solve them. Many questions do not have "right" answers. You may have to make some mistakes in order to succeed. In fact, the "trial and error" method is often the best one!

A. Choose the problem that most interests you from the list below. Circle the number of the problem you select.

1. You own a variety store. One day you find a huge box of hula hoops in the basement. You haven't sold a hula hoop in a long time. What can you do with this supply of hoops so they won't be a total loss?

2. It is Friday. Your teacher announces a math test on Tuesday. The boss at your part-time job asks you to work late on Monday night. You need the time to study, but you know that your boss really counts on you to work. How can you meet your responsibilities to your boss *and* to your studies?

3. You have won three tickets to a concert. You have three equally good friends who are all music fans. You only have enough tickets to take two of them to the show. Which two friends will you invite?

4. You have to draw the diagram at the bottom of this page without lifting your pencil from the page or retracing a line. It can be done, but how will you do it?

B. On the back of the sheet, *describe at least one strategy* you could use to solve the problem you chose in *Part A*. (Don't actually solve the problem now. You'll get a chance to do that in the next section.)

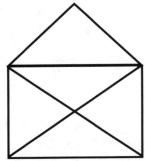

C. What is your *solution* to the problem you selected in *Part A*? Describe the solution on the back of this sheet.

LEARNING FROM GRAPHICS: THE DIAGRAM

Sometimes you will find information visually presented in a *graphic* or chart. A *diagram* is one commonly used type of graphic. A diagram provides a *picture* to make details easier to understand.

A. The diagram to the right shows which parts of the brain control the things a person does. Use information from the diagram to answer the questions below.

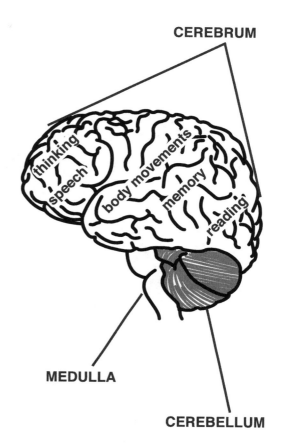

1. What part of your brain controls body movements?

   _____

2. What four other body functions are controlled by this part of the brain?

   _____

   _____

   _____

   _____

3. Name two more parts of the brain.

   _____

   _____

B. Read the paragraph below. Then draw a diagram that makes the details clear. Draw your diagram on the back of this sheet.

> Scientists know that Earth, from its surface to its center, is made up of layers of rock. The top layer, called the *crust*, is the thinnest layer. It is solid rock. The middle layer is the mantle. The mantle is made up of very hot rock. In fact, some of the mantle is partly melted. The deepest layer, the core, is at the very center of Earth. No one has been able to dig to Earth's core. But scientists think it is made up of hot, heavy rocks and minerals.

LEARNING FROM GRAPHICS: MORE PRACTICE USING A DIAGRAM

Information often becomes clearer once you look at a *diagram*.

A. Read the paragraph below. Then answer the questions that follow.

> There are eight planets in our solar system. Mercury is the nearest to the sun. Venus, Earth, Mars, Jupiter, Saturn, Uranus, and Neptune follow in that order. The planets vary greatly in size, but all are smaller than the sun. The smallest is Mercury. Next, according to size, are Mars, Venus, Earth, Neptune, Uranus, Saturn, and, the largest planet, Jupiter.

1. Which two planets are closest to Earth?

   _____

2. Which two planets are the largest? _____

3. How do the planets compare in size to the sun? _____

B. Now look at the diagram of the planets. Use the diagram to answer the questions that follow.

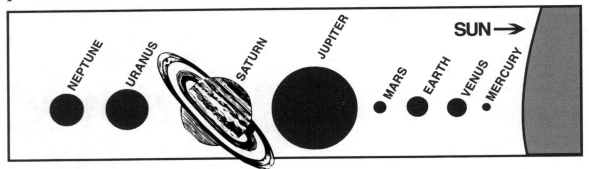

1. Which two planets are farthest from the sun?

   _____

2. Which planet is about the same size as Earth? _____

3. Which planet is farthest from the sun? Which is nearest?

   _____

C. Write your answers to the following items on the back of this sheet.

1. Was it easier to answer questions using the diagram or the paragraph? Explain why.

2. How is Saturn different from all the other planets? Tell where you found the information needed to answer this question.

LEARNING FROM GRAPHICS: Using Tables

A *table* organizes information and shows it in graphic form. Most tables have *rows,* which run from left to right. They also have *columns,* which run from top to bottom. A table allows you to find details quickly.

A. The following table gives details about the first U.S. presidents. Use facts in the table to answer the questions.

PRESIDENT	DATES IN OFFICE	POLITICAL PARTY	VICE-PRESIDENT
1. George Washington	1789–1797	Federalist	John Adams
2. John Adams	1797–1801	Federalist	Thomas Jefferson
3. Thomas Jefferson	1801–1809	Democratic Republican	Aaron Burr George Clinton
4. James Madison	1809–1817	Democratic Republican	George Clinton Elbridge Gerry
5. John Quincy Adams	1825–1829	Democratic Republican	John C. Calhoun

1. Name two men who served both as vice-president and as president of the United States.

   _____ and _____

2. Who served as vice-president under Thomas Jefferson *and* under James Madison? _____

3. What year did a Democratic Republican first become president? _____

B. Read the following paragraph. On the back of this sheet, make a table to show the same information.

   The cost of living has climbed throughout the last half of this century. The price of food, for example, rose steadily. In 1950, a quart of milk cost $.21. By 1960, the price had gone up to $.26. In 1970 a quart cost $.33, and in 1980 it cost $.41. By 1990, that quart of milk had jumped to $.83! The cost of coffee rose, too. In 1950 a pound cost $.55; in 1960, $.75; in 1970, $.91; in 1980, $1.09, and in 1990, $3.50. The price of bread also soared. In 1950, a loaf cost just $.14. In 1960, it cost $.20. Bread was $.24 a loaf in 1970 and $.36 a loaf in 1980. By 1990, it took about $1.49 to buy a loaf of bread.

LEARNING FROM GRAPHICS: Previewing and Reading Tables

You can *preview* a table by studying its title and headings. They will tell you what kind of information the table includes. Then you can read the table for details.

A. Preview the table. Circle a letter to show which item correctly completes each sentence below.   ○

**STUDENT ATHLETIC PARTICIPATION
LINCOLN HIGH SCHOOL—FALL 2007**

SPORT	MALES	FEMALES	TOTAL
volleyball	0	25	25
soccer	18	17	35
football	29	1	30
cross country	29	23	52
all fall sports	**76**	**66**	**142**

1. This table gives information about the:
   a. types of sports Lincoln High offers throughout the year.
   b. number of students who participated in various fall sports.
   c. costs of the Lincoln High athletic program.

2. The first column lists the:
   a. fall sports at Lincoln High.
   b. high schools in the city.
   c. number of female athletes who played fall sports.

3. Information in this chart will allow you to:
   a. compare fall athletic participation of males and females.
   b. compare the popularity of the different fall sports.
   c. compare both participation and popularity.

B. Read the table again. Use the details to answer these questions on the back of this sheet.

   1. What is the most popular fall sport at Lincoln High?
   2. Which sport has only female athletes?
   3. Which two sports are equally popular with males and females?

C. *Scan* the table for the answer to the following question. Write your answer on the back of this sheet.

   Jenny was the kicker on the 2007 Lincoln High football team. How many other girls were on that team?

LEARNING FROM GRAPHICS: USING A BAR GRAPH

Bar graphs make it easy to *visually* compare details. The topic of the graph below is the same as the table in the last exercise. You will notice that the table gave more specific numbers—but the bar graph emphasizes the comparisons.

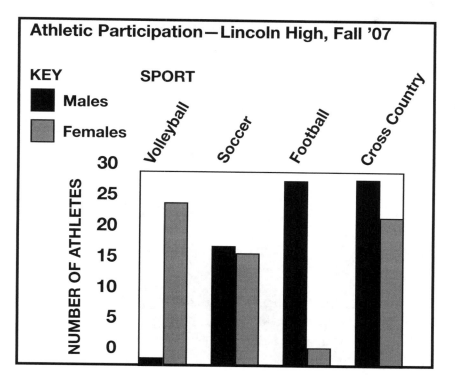

A. Study the bar graph above. Circle the word or words that correctly complete each sentence.

1. Volleyball is the (most / least) popular fall sport for Lincoln High females.

2. In the fall of '07, (more / fewer) Lincoln High women played volleyball than men.

3. (Cross country / Soccer) had nearly equal numbers of female and male players.

4. You would find the fewest players in the women's locker room after a (football / soccer) game.

B. Take the role of a reporter on the Lincoln High student newspaper. Write an article based on information in the graph. You could write a straight *news article* that just reports facts. Or, you could write an *editorial* that gives your opinion based on the facts. Write your article on the back of this sheet.

LEARNING FROM GRAPHICS: Using a Line Graph

Line graphs show change over a period of time.

A. The line graph below shows information about Lincoln High's student population over five years. Read the graph to answer the questions.

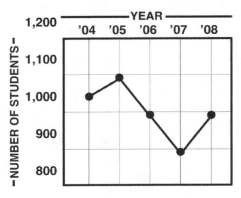

1. How many students went to Lincoln High in 2006? _____

2. In what year was Lincoln's student body largest ? _____

3. What happened to the Lincoln High population in 2007?

   _____

4. When Lincoln's student body was largest, how large was it? _____

B. Line graphs can also compare the development of two similar items. Study the graph below. It compares the student population of Lincoln High, a city school, with that of Lakeridge High, a suburban school. Read the graph to answer the questions.

1. How many students went to Lakeridge in 2004? _____

2. Which school had the most students in 2005?

   _____

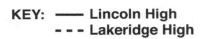

3. When did both schools have the same number of students?

   _____

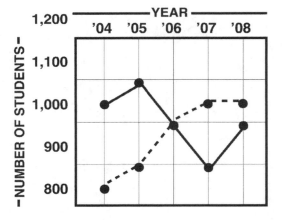

4. Which school's population saw the steadiest growth?

   _____

C. Describe what seems to be happening to the populations of Lincoln and Lakeridge High in 2008. Write your answer on the back of this sheet.

LEARNING FROM GRAPHICS: Using a Circle Graph

Look at the example of a *circle graph* below. You can see that this type of graph, sometimes called a *pie graph*, is named for its shape. The circle stands for the whole of something—100 percent of it. The parts of the circle (or slices of the pie) stand for the parts of the whole. Circle graphs show the size of the parts. They let the reader compare the parts to one another and to the whole.

A. This circle graph represents the contents of an average city garbage dump in 2000. Read the graph to fill in the blanks.

1. _____ percent of the garbage came from yard debris.

2. _____ percent of the garbage came from food wastes.

3. The least amount of garbage came from

   _____.

4. The recycling of

   _____

   would *most* reduce the amount of garbage in the dump.

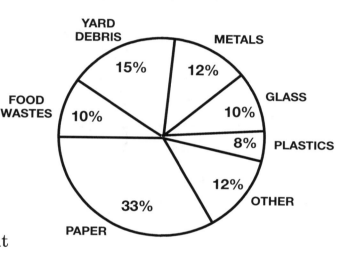

AT THE DUMP—2000

B. Put a **check** (✓) by information you can get from the graph above.

1. ____ a comparison of the amounts of different products that filled an average city dump

2. ____ a comparison of the contents of dumps in several cities

3. ____ changes in garbage dump contents over several years

4. ____ the recycling habits of an average American family

C. On the back of this sheet, make a circle graph showing how you spend a typical weekday. One section, for example, could represent the number of hours you spend sleeping. Other sections might include time spent on studies, watching TV, with friends, at school, at your job, on grooming, on the phone, and so on.

LEARNING FROM GRAPHICS: Using a Picture Graph

A *picture graph*, or *pictograph*, uses pictures to stand for a certain number of something. Picture graphs usually do not give exact numbers. Instead, they round off amounts to the nearest units. A picture graph clearly shows how the amounts *compare* to each other.

A. Study the picture graph. Then write **T** or **F** to show whether each statement below is **true** or **false**.

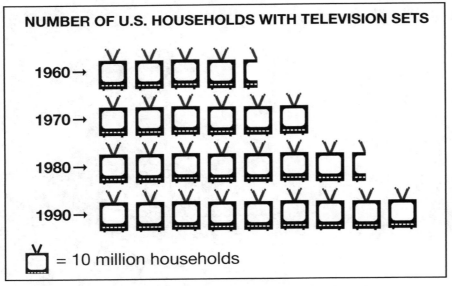

NUMBER OF U.S. HOUSEHOLDS WITH TELEVISION SETS

1960 →
1970 →
1980 →
1990 →

= 10 million households

1. ____ There were no television sets in the United States in 1960.

2. ____ The number of households with TV sets rose steadily between 1960 and 1990.

3. ____ In 1980, about 75 million households had TV sets.

4. ____ The picture graph compares the number of U.S. households that had TV sets over four decades.

5. ____ Television ownership dropped off sharply in 1980.

6. ____ The graph shows that TV become less popular over time.

B. Look at the items you marked **false** in *Part A*. On the back of this sheet, rewrite those statements to make them **true**.

C. Make a picture graph on the back of this sheet. Select one of the subjects below, or choose one of your own:

1. the number of students in various classes

2. the amount of money you earned at different jobs

3. the number of people in the families of friends

THE VOCABULARY OF MAPS

Do you need to study a world map in your textbook? Look at a park map in a guidebook to find a picnic area? Use a road map to find a friend's house? Knowing certain terms will help you whenever you need to read a map.

A. Use a word from the box to complete each sentence.

symbols	**compass rose**	**borders**
legend	**location key**	**scale**

1. Map makers often draw a _____ _____ to show directions on a map. This design will always show North (N), and it may show all eight directions *(North, Northeast, East, Southeast, South, Southwest, West, and Northwest)*. A typical example is on the right.

2. _____ are boundary lines that mark where a certain area stops and another begins. The lines between states are an example.

3. _____ are little symbols that stand for something on a map. For example, a star (★) often stands for a capital city.

4. The _____ is a key to the size and distance shown on a map. It usually shows distances in miles and looks something like this:

   0   10
   |—————————|
   1 inch stands for 10 miles

5. The _____ explains what the map symbols mean. It looks something like this:

---- national boundaries	● major cities	
—— county boundaries	★ capitals	
--- state boundaries		

6. The letters and numbers along the sides of the map are called the _____. The letters appear at the top and bottom of the map. The numbers appear on the sides. The reader uses both letters and numbers as guides to a specific location.

B. On the back of this sheet, design your own compass rose. Put in all eight directions.

USING A MAP

The *legend* tells what each *symbol* on the map means.

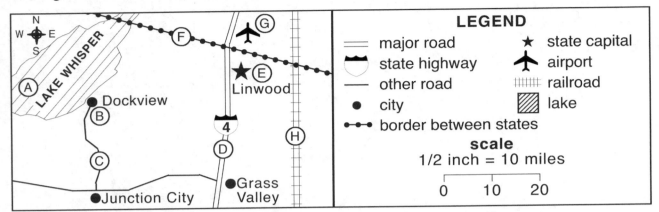

A. Notice the letters beside some of the symbols on the map. Tell the meaning of each symbol by writing a letter beside each word below.

1. ____ city
2. ____ capital
3. ____ lake
4. ____ border between states

5. ____ state highway
6. ____ smaller road
7. ____ railroad
8. ____ airport

B. Circle the word that correctly completes each sentence.

1. (Grass Valley / Dockview) is on Lake Whisper's southeastern shore.
2. Highway 4 (does / does not) cross a state border.
3. Linwood is a (capital city / airport).
4. An airport is just (north / south) of the state border.
5. Railroad tracks run (along / across) the state border.

C. Circle the letter of the correct answer.

1. If you take the state highway south from the capital, you'll come to:
   a. Linwood   b. Junction City   c. Grass Valley   d. Dockview

2. Which mode of travel could take you across the state border?
   a. boat   b. automobile   c. train   d. all of the above

3. About how far is it from Grass Valley to Linwood?
   a. 100 miles   b. 1,000 miles   c. 20 miles   d. 2 miles

D. Imagine that a friend is arriving at the airport, renting a car, and driving to Dockview. Write route directions on the back of this sheet.

     Study Skills 1 • © Saddleback Educational Publishing • www.sdlback.com

TWO TYPES OF MAPS

Different kinds of maps have different purposes. They can show the floor plan of a single room or the shape of the whole world. *Physical maps* show land levels and landforms such as hills, mountains, and valleys. *Colors or shading* are often used as symbols. Blue usually stands for water. Green often shows lowlands, while brown shows highlands.

Political maps show borders of countries and states. They identify cities and towns. Political maps reflect changes made by people. Some maps include both physical landforms *and* political boundaries.

A. The two maps below are of the same area. Compare the maps by circling the word that best completes each statement.

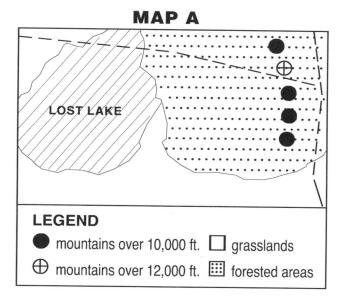

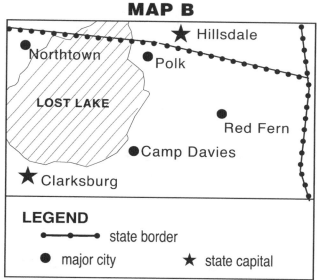

1. *Map A* is a (physical / political) map.

2. *Map B is* a (physical / political) map.

3. A state border is just north of (Polk / Clarksburg).

4. (Camp Davies / Clarksburg) is a state capital.

5. Hillsdale and Red Fern (are / are not) in the same state.

6. A mountain range runs (east / west) of Lost Lake.

B. Draw the outline of an imaginary island on the back of this sheet. Make a map that shows both physical and political features of your island. Use colors or shading to identify land forms (mountains, valleys, forests, and so on). Mark cities and towns. Make a legend for your map.

USING GRAPHIC AIDS: A Review

Graphics are valuable study aids. They can help you picture information in a way that is easier to understand, use, and remember.

A. Write a letter to match the name of each graphic with its example.

a. diagram	**b.** table	**c.** bar graph	**d.** line graph
e. circle graph	**f.** picture graph	**g.** map	

1. ____   THE ZESTO FIVE-IN-ONE

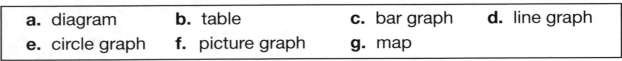

back scratcher, potato peeler, can opener, pocket-knife, barbecue lighter

2. ____   ZESTO SALES AREAS

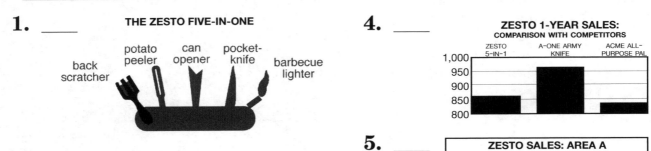

3. ____   PRODUCT SPECIFICATIONS

PARTS		PRICE	AVAILABILITY
ZESTO FIVE-IN-ONE	can opener, potato peeler, barbecue lighter, back scratcher, pocketknife	$8.99	stores, catalogs, door-to-door
A-ONE ARMY KNIFE	can opener, hunting knife, camping knife, nail file	$34.99	catalogs only
ACME ALL-PURPOSE PAL	can opener, nail file, alarm clock, pocket-knife	$14.98	stores only

4. ____   ZESTO 1-YEAR SALES: COMPARISON WITH COMPETITORS

ZESTO 5-IN-1   A-ONE ARMY KNIFE   ACME ALL-PURPOSE PAL
1,000 / 950 / 900 / 850 / 800

5. ____   ZESTO SALES: AREA A

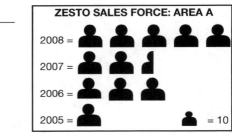

sold door-to-door — 10%
sold by phone — 15%
sold through catalogs — 25%
sold in stores — 50%

6. ____   ZESTO SALES FORCE: AREA A

2008 =
2007 =
2006 =
2005 =   = 10

7. ____   ZESTO SEASONAL SALES

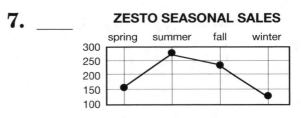

spring   summer   fall   winter
300 / 250 / 200 / 150 / 100

B. Read the paragraph below. On the back of this sheet, show the details in a graphic. Choose the graphic form you think best pictures the material.

> In the 1930s, Americans faced the Great Depression. As the '30s began, just over 9 percent of American workers were unemployed. By 1931, the unemployment rate had climbed to almost 16 percent. Jobs continued to disappear as the Great Depression worsened. In 1932, the number of jobless Americans rose to 24 percent. In 1933, the unemployment rate peaked—one-quarter of America's workers were without jobs!

ANSWER KEY

1 A LEARNING SKILLS INVENTORY

Answers will vary.

2 STUDY SKILLS VOCABULARY

A. 1.h 2.j 3.i 4.b 5.a 6.d 7.f 8.g
9.e 10.c

B.

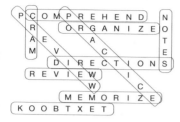

3 A GOOD STUDY ENVIRONMENT

Answers will vary.

4 TIME MANAGEMENT: Tracking Your Time

Answers will vary.

5 TIME MANAGEMENT: Planning Your Time

Answers will vary.

6 THINKING ABOUT LEARNING STYLE

Answers will vary.

7 IDENTIFYING YOUR LEARNING STYLE

A. 1.V 2.K 3.V 4.K 5.K 6.V 7.A 8.A
9.A 10.V

B. kinesthetic

C. Answers will vary.

8 KNOW YOUR INSTRUCTOR

Answers will vary.

9 SETTING GOALS

Answers will vary.

10 IMPROVING MEMORY

Answers will vary.

11 TWO WAYS TO IMPROVE MEMORY

Answers will vary.

A. Group names will vary.

— *Things in a bathroom:* sink, bathtub, mirror, shower, toilet

— *Transportation:* bus, airplane, subway, steamship, truck

— *Fruits:* banana, orange, peach, apple, grapefruit

B., C. Answers will vary.

12 MNEMONICS: Memory Boosters

Answers will vary.

13 TEXTBOOKS: Special Features

A. 1.f 2.b 3.a 4.d 5.g 6.e 7.c

B. 1.title page 2.copyright page 3.table of contents 4.index 5.glossary
6.index

14 TEXTBOOKS: The First Few Pages

A. 1.Exploring United States History
2.Will Wilson & Bev Booth 3.Masters Publishing Company 4.Buffalo, New York

B. Answers will vary but should approximate: 1.The legal right to be the only publisher, producer, or seller of a piece of writing, music, or art. 2.To make sure the information is up-to-date.

C. 1.© 2., 3.Answers will vary.

D. Should include title, author, publisher, and place of publication.

15 TEXTBOOKS: Using the Table of Contents

A. 1.F 2.T 3.F 4.T 5.F 6.F 7.F 8.T
9.T 10.F

B. Circle 3, 4, and 6.

C. Answers will vary.

16 TEXTBOOKS: Using the Index

A. 1.TOC 2.I 3.TOC 4.I 5.I 6.TOC
7.TOC 8.I

B. Alphabetical order is: 1. abolitionists
2. anti-slavery movement 3. Barton, Clara 4. Bull Run, Battle of 5. Confederacy
6. Davis, Jefferson 7. Gettysburg, Battle of 8. Grant, Ulysses S. 9. Lee, Robert E. 10. Lincoln, Abraham
11. Reconstruction period 12. women in the war

17 TEXTBOOKS: Using Chapter Clues

A. 1.b 2.a 3.c 4.c 5.a

B., C. Answers will vary.

18 TEXTBOOKS: The Glossary

A. 1.a 2.b 3.b

B. Alphabetical order is: 1. active
2. erupt 3. fertile 4. geothermal
5. sulfur 6. volcanoes

C. Answers will vary.

19 UNDERSTANDING YOUR TEXTBOOK: A Puzzle

Crossword puzzle:
- 4 across: TITLEPAGE
- 5 across: ALPHABET
- 8 across: TABLEOFCONTENTS
- 9 (down at C): CONTENTS
- 10 across: APPENDIX
- 1 down: BIOGRAPHY
- 2 down: COPYRIGHT
- 3 down: QUESTION
- 6 down: GLOSSARY
- 7 down: INDEX
- CHAPTER (down)

20 SKIMMING AND SCANNING

A. 1. c 2. a 3. b

B. Answers will vary.

C. 1881

21 MORE SKIMMING PRACTICE

Answers will vary.

A. *Circle* title. Underline first sentence. *Main idea* answers will vary.

B. *Circle* title and subheadings. *Underline* first sentence. *Main idea* answers will vary.

22 SCANNING PRACTICE

1. 690-4432 2. 62 3. Sports Chat
4. 1847 5. $.05

23 THE LIBRARY: Words to Know

A. 1. f 2. g 3. e 4. h 5. c 6. a 7. j 8. d
9. b 10. i

B. 1. (reference book)/not a person
2. (periodical)/not a place 3. (bar code)/
not a type of book 4. (fiction)/not a true
account based on facts

24 THE LIBRARY: Fiction and Nonfiction

A. 1. F 2. NF 3. NF 4. F 5. NF

B. 1. 4 2. 1 3. 3 4. 5 5. 2

C. 1. c 2. a 3. b

25 THE LIBRARY: The Dewey Decimal System

A. 1. 700–799, Fine Arts 2. 900–999,
History 3. 400–499, Languages
4. 600–699, Technology

B. 1. b 2. b

C. Correct order: Forecasting…, Big
Birds…, The Stamp…, Astounding…

26 THE LIBRARY: Call Numbers

A. 1. spine 2. juvenile fiction 3. author
4. Dewey decimal number 5. fiction

B. Correct Order: 519 COO, 519 TRE, 759 ADA, 795
WEB

C. 519 COO (Science), 519 TRE (Science),
759 ADA (Fine Arts), 795 WEB (Fine Arts)

27 THE LIBRARY: Using the Card Catalog

A. 1. author, P 2. subject, T 3. subject, A
4. title, H 5. title, V

B. 1. Heat from the Heavens 2. Dennis Wong
3. solar heat 4. 921.7 WON 5. 123 6.
nonfiction; because it has a Dewey decimal
number

28 THE COMPUTERIZED CATALOG

Crossword puzzle:
- 3 across: AUTHOR
- 4 across: CALL
- 6 across: TITLE
- 8 across: SUBJECT
- 1 down: PUBLISHER
- 2 down: COLLATION
- 5 down: LOCATION
- 4 down: CONTROL
- 7 down: MENU

29 THE LIBRARY: Skills Review

A. 1. branch 2. computerized catalog 3. menu
4. subject 5. titles 6. Dewey decimal number

B.

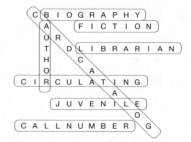

30 REFERENCE: Information Resources

A. 1. f 2. g 3. b 4. c 5. h 6. a 7. e 8. d

B. 1. dictionary 2. atlas 3. biographical
reference 4. Readers' Guide to Periodical
Literature

C. Answers will vary.

31 REFERENCE: Alphabetical Order

A. 2. k 3. g 4. n 5. r 6. m 7. x 8. s 9. d
10. c

B. 2. vwxyz 3. pqrst 4. ijklm 5. defgh 6. abcde

C. 1. 5, 3, 1, 4, 2 2. 5, 2, 1, 4, 3 3. 2, 1, 5, 4, 3

D. 2. Farmer McDonald only picks ripe tomatoes.
3. Bob bought fresh fruit near Newark.
4. Many merry motorcyclists motored near the water.

32 MORE ALPHABETIZING PRACTICE

A. 1. bird 2. medicine 3. gold 4. radish

B. 1. Louis Armstrong 2. Cesar Chavez
3. Amelia Earhart 4. Albert Einstein 5. Gerald Ford 6. Henry Ford 7. Marilyn Monroe
8. Sandra Day O'Connor 9. Elvis Presley
10. Babe Ruth 11. Booker T. Washington
12. George Washington

C. 1. Pacific Ocean 2. Thomas Paine 3. Poland
4. pyramid

D. 1. grandchild 2. grandparent 3. granny
4. granola 5. grape

33 REFERENCE: Dictionary Guide Words

A. hurdle, hunter, husband, husk, hurry, hurricane

B. 1. b 2. d 3. e 4. c 5. a

C. 1. on 2. after 3. on 4. after 5. before
6. after 7. after 8. on 9. before

D. Answers will vary.

34 REFERENCE: Dictionary Definitions

A. 1. to smear with grease 2. melted animal fat
3. any soft, oily substance, especially one that is put on the moving parts of machines to make them run smoothly

B., C. Answers will vary.

35 REFERENCE: A Dictionary Tells Parts of Speech

A. 2. n., v. 3. n., v. 4. adj., v. 5. adj., adv. 6. n., v. 7. v., adj. 8. adj., v. 9. n., v. 10. n., v., adj.

B. 1. a 2. b 3. c 4. b 5. a

C. Answers will vary.

36 REFERENCE: More Dictionary Information

A. 1. sen•sa•tion 2. sight 3. hear•ing 4. o•dor
5. vi•brate 6. taste•less

B. 1. mēt 2. mōl′dē 3. wĭn 4. mōst′lē 5. snāk
6. chĭm′nē

C. If I called the wrong number, what did you answer for?

37 DICTIONARY REVIEW

A. 2. b 3. e 4. c 5. a 6. d 7. b 8. c

B. Answers will vary.

38 REFERENCE: The Encyclopedia

A. 1. T 2. F 3. T 4. T 5. F 6. F

B. 1. 8 2. 9 3. 2 4. 9 5. 10 6. 4

C. Answers will vary.

39 REFERENCE: The World Atlas

A. Check (✓) 1, 2, and 5.

B. 1. 46 2. B4 3. Kansas

C. Answers will vary.

40 REFERENCE: The Thesaurus

A. Answers will vary.

B. 1. a 2. b 3. b 4. a

C. Answers will vary.

41 REFERENCE: The Readers' Guide to Periodical Literature

A. 1. 29–32 2. July 2007 3. The Philippines: Islands of Unrest 4. T. Newcomb 5. *World News Today*

B. Magazine: Modern Medicine, Date: Feb/12/07, Volume: 31

C. Answers will vary.

42 REFERENCE: Almanacs

A. 1. 196 2. 614 3. 357 4. 523 5. 197

B. Check (✓) 1, 4, and 6.

C. Answers will vary.

43 REFERENCE: Biographical Dictionaries

A. 1. b 2. e 3. a 4. c 5. d

B. 1. painters 2. authors 3. astronauts
4. explorers 5. First Ladies

C. Answers will vary.

44 REFERENCE REVIEW: A Scavenger Hunt

A. 1. AT 2. BD 3. RG 4. D 5. AL 6. BD
7. E 8. AL 9. E 10. D 11. D 12. T
13. AT 14. AL 15. RG

B. Answers will vary.

45 REFERENCE: The Bibliography

A. 1. alphabetical order 2. indented
3. enclosed in quotation marks
4. underlined 5. topic 6. colon
7. period

B. Answers will vary.

46 FOLLOWING WRITTEN DIRECTIONS

A. The answers for 1, 3, and 5 should be written *under* the answer blank. Questions 2, 4, and 6 should *not* be answered. 1. student's name 3. 7:00 A.M. 5. independence of America

B. *None* of the questions should be answered. Only the student's name should be written on the back of the sheet.

47 FOLLOWING SPOKEN DIRECTIONS

   A. 1. The student's name should be in the *upper left-hand corner* and the *last letter of last name left off.*
2. dashes in current date 3. 12
4. Circle 20. 5. Draw a *star.*
6. any number *except 6*

   B. Answers will vary.

48 TAKING NOTES FROM READING: Mapping

   Answers will vary.

49 TAKING NOTES FROM READING: More Mapping Practice

   Answers will vary.

50 TAKING NOTES FROM READING: Outlining

   Answers will vary.

51 TAKING NOTES FROM READING: More Outlining Practice

   Answers will vary.

52 STREAMLINING YOUR NOTES

   A. 1. c 2. d 3. f 4. a 5. e 6. b

   B. 1. = 2. etc. 3. dept. 4. 4

   C. Answers will vary.

53 TAKING NOTES WHILE LISTENING

   A. 1. F 2. T 3. F 4. T

   B., C. Answers will vary.

54 ACTIVE LISTENING

   Answers will vary.

55 MORE HINTS FOR ACTIVE LISTENING

   A. 1. + 2. – 3. + 4. – 5. +

   B. Check (✓) 2, 3, and 4.

   C. the following problems, First of all, Secondly, and Most importantly

56 NOTE TAKING: Paraphrasing Information

   Answers will vary.

57 NOTE TAKING: Recognizing Relevant and Irrelevant Information

   A. 1. a 2. d 3. c 4. c

   B. Circle 1.

   C. Circle 5.

58 NOTE TAKING REVIEW

   A. 1. mapping 2. outlining
3. abbreviations 4. paraphrase
5. symbols

   B. notes

59 USING CONTEXT TO CLUE MEANING

   A. 1. b 2. c 3. b 4. a

   B. 1. c 2. c 3. b 4. a

   C. Answers will vary.

60 CONTEXT CLUES: Definition

   A. 2. speak two languages 3. dark yellow color
4. avocado 5. unable to pay his debts

   B. 1. complete change 2. baby frog 3. hairy worm 4. hard shell

   C. Answers will vary.

61 CONTEXT CLUES: Examples

   A. 1. a 2. b 3. a 4. c 5. c

   B., C. Answers will vary.

62 CONTEXT CLUES: Comparison or Contrast

   A. 2. contrast 3. comparison 4. contrast
5. contrast 6. comparison 7. comparison

   B. In *Part A,* circle: 1. as, as 2. Although 3. like
4. but 5. While 6. as, as 7. similar to

   C. Answers will vary.

63 USING CONTEXT TO CLUE MEANING: A Review

   A. 1. example 2. contrast 3. definition
4. comparison 5. contrast

   B. 1. c 2. d 3. b 4. a 5. e

   C. Answers will vary.

64 A MATTER OF CONTEXT

   A. 1. b 2. a 3. b 4. a 5. a 6. b

   B. Answers will vary.

65 UNLOCKING WORD MEANING: Prefixes, Suffixes, and Roots

   A. 1. <u>color</u>less 2. <u>home</u>less 3. <u>pre</u>pay 4. <u>joy</u>ful
5. <u>count</u>ing 6. dis<u>count</u>ed 7. re<u>call</u>ed
8. <u>pre</u>view 9. <u>freez</u>er 10. <u>strang</u>er
11. <u>health</u>ful 12. un<u>healthy</u>

   B. 1. a 2. b 3. b

   C. Answers will vary.

66 UNLOCKING WORD MEANING: Prefixes

   A. 2. <u>bi</u>cycle, b 3. <u>non</u>sense, a 4. <u>super</u>human, a

   B. 2. X 3. pre+flight 4. X 5. X 6. in+visible
7. mis+behave 8. X

   C. 2. bicycle, tricycle 3. preview, review

   D. Answers will vary.

67 UNLOCKING WORD MEANING: Suffixes

   A. 1. formation 2. location 3. tourists
4. Swimmers 5. pollution

   B. 1. cleverest 2. higher 3. smarter 4. strangest

   C. Answers will vary.

68 WORD PARTS: Check Your Understanding

A. 2. relax+ation, a   3. semi+awake, b
4. bi+month+ly, b   5. de+caffein(e)+ate, a
6. re+material+ized, b

B. Answers will vary.

69 BETTER COMPREHENSION: Key Words and Ideas

A. Answers may vary slightly, but should approximate: 2. police stopped robbers' car headed south on Highway 101   3. be on time or early for work   4. soccer tryouts Wednesday 7:00 P.M. Dawson Park   5. bring rain gear camping—forecast showers, wind

B. Answers will vary.

70 IMPROVING UNDERSTANDING: Recognizing Sequence

A. 2. chores: shopping for groceries, preparing dinner, washing dishes   3. party preparations: buying supplies, blowing up balloons, decorating room

B. 3, 1, 2, 5, 4, 6

C. Answers will vary.

71 PREPARING FOR TESTS

A. Answers will vary.

B. 1. T   2. F   3. T   4. F   5. F   6. T   7. T   8. F

C. Answers will vary.

72 THE TERMINOLOGY OF TESTS

A.

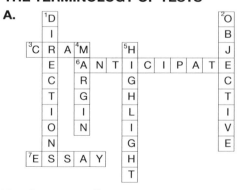

B. Answers will vary.

73 TEST-TAKING TIPS

A. Answers will vary.

B. 1. b   2. a   3. b   4. b

C. Answers will vary.

74 TAKING A TRUE/FALSE TEST

A. 1. T   2. F   3. F   4. T   5. T   6. F

B. 1. 2, 6   2. false

75 TAKING A TRUE/FALSE TEST: More Practice

A. 1. T   2. F   3. T   4. F

B. 1. F   2. T   3. T   4. F   5. T   6. F   7. F

C. Answers will vary.

76 TAKING A MULTIPLE CHOICE TEST

A. 1. c   2. c   3. b

B. Answers will vary.

77 TAKING A MULTIPLE CHOICE TEST: More Practice

A. 1. a, c   2. e, a   3. a, b   4. e, a   5. a, b

B. 1. c   2. b   3. c   4. a

78 TAKING A COMPLETION TEST

A. 1. iris   2. pupil   3. light rays   4. optic nerve   5. brain

B. Answers will vary.

79 TAKING A COMPLETION TEST: More Practice

A. 1. blank   2. context   3. an   4. guess

B. 1. explorer   2. four   3. mail   4. airplane

C. 1. 1492   2. c   3. 30   4. February

D. Answers will vary.

80 TAKING A MATCHING TEST

A. 1. c   2. a   3. d   4. b

B. 1. e   2. g   3. b   4. c   5. d   6. a   7. f

C. Answers will vary.

81 TAKING OBJECTIVE TESTS: A Review

A. 1. F   2. F   3. T

B. 1. b   2. a

C. 1. false   2. true

D. 1. a   2. c   3. b

82 THE VOCABULARY OF ESSAY TESTS

A. 1. Describe   2. Discuss   3. Summarize
4. Explain   5. Compare

B. Answers will vary.

83 THE VOCABULARY OF ESSAY TESTS: More Practice

A.

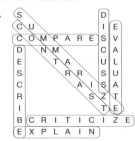

B. 1. a   2. b   3. b   4. a

84 TAKING AN ESSAY TEST

   A. 2. a   3. b   4. a

   B. Answers will vary.

85 TAKING AN ESSAY TEST:
Further Hints

   Answers will vary.

86 REVIEWING YOUR TEST

   A. Student reviews test.

   B. 1. a   2. b

   C. Answers will vary.

87 THREE STEPS TO
SOLVING PROBLEMS

   Answers will vary.

88 PROBLEM-SOLVING PRACTICE

   Answers will vary.

89 LEARNING FROM GRAPHICS:
The Diagram

   A. 1. cerebrum   2. thinking, speech,
      memory, reading   3. medulla, cerebellum

   B. Answers will vary.

90 LEARNING FROM GRAPHICS: More
Practice Using a Diagram

   A. 1. Venus and Mars   2. Saturn and Jupiter
      3. smaller

   B. 1. Neptune and Uranus   2. Venus
      3. Neptune, Mercury

   C. Answers will vary.

91 LEARNING FROM GRAPHICS:
Using Tables

   A. 1. John Adams, Thomas Jefferson
      2. George Clinton   3. 1801

   B. Answers will vary.

92 LEARNING FROM GRAPHICS:
Previewing and Reading Tables

   A. 1. b   2. a   3. c

   B. 1. cross country   2. volleyball
      3. soccer and cross country

   C. 0

93 LEARNING FROM GRAPHICS:
Using a Bar Graph

   A. 1. most   2. more   3. Soccer   4. football

   B. Answers will vary.

94 LEARNING FROM GRAPHICS:
Using a Line Graph

   A. 1. 1,000   2. 2005   3. It dropped.
      4. 1,100

   B. 1. 850   2. Lincoln   3. 2006
      4. Lakeridge

   C. Answers will vary.

95 LEARNING FROM GRAPHICS:
Using a Circle Graph

   A. 1. 15   2. 10   3. plastics   4. paper

   B. Check (✓) 1.

   C. Answers will vary.

96 LEARNING FROM GRAPHICS:
Using a Picture Graph

   A. 1. F   2. T   3. T   4. T   5. F   6. F

   B., C. Answers will vary.

97 THE VOCABULARY OF MAPS

   A. 1. compass rose   2. Borders
      3. Symbols   4. scale   5. legend
      6. location key

   B. Answers will vary.

98 USING A MAP

   A. 1. B   2. E   3. A   4. F   5. D   6. C
      7. H   8. G

   B. 1. Dockview   2. does   3. capital city
      4. north   5. across

   C. 1. c   2. d   3. c

   D. Answers will vary.

99 TWO TYPES OF MAPS

   A. 1. physical   2. political   3. Polk   4.
      Clarksburg
      5. are not   6. east

   B. Answers will vary.

100 USING GRAPHIC AIDS: A Review

   A. 1. a   2. g   3. b   4. c   5. e   6. f   7. d

   B. Answers will vary.